# CATHEDRALS OF THE MOVIES

# CATHEDRALS OF THE MOVIES

A History of British
Cinemas and their
Audiences

## DAVID ATWELL

THE ARCHITECTURAL PRESS: LONDON

First published in 1980 by
The Architectural Press Ltd:
London

Paperback edition 1981

© David Atwell 1980

ISBN 0 85139 773 5

*Frontispiece*
Designed by E. Norman Bailey
in 1931, the auditorium of the
Regal, Uxbridge is a
full-blooded espousal of art
deco detailing

Set in Palatino
Printed in Great Britain by
Mackays of Chatham Limited

To my mother, who took me to so many
cinemas for the first time

————————————

# CONTENTS

**The architecture of the Movie Palace was a triumph of suppressed desire.**

BEN HALL in 'The Best Remaining Seats' 1961

# FOREWORD

by
**Bevis Hillier**
**Chairman, The Thirties Society**

No kings or emperors have ever wandered through more luxurious surroundings. In a sense these theatres are a social valve in that the public can partake of the same luxuries as the rich, and use them to the same full extent!

HAROLD RAMBUSCH in 'American theatres of today', 1929

THE Odeon, Redhill, Surrey, does not get star billing in David Atwell's book. It was designed by Andrew Mather in 1938, which was Mather's busiest year – the year he designed eleven Odeons for Oscar Deutsch. In its latest avatar as Busby's Club, it is certainly not a building one would travel half-way from London to Brighton to see.

Yet the white-tiled exterior of the Redhill Odeon, with its characteristic tower set apart from the main building like the bell-tower of a Greek church, and even more its interior, which formerly contained streamlined detailing, chrome-armed sofas and column ashtrays, were my first insight into the period before my birth, with that chronological voyeurism which is the beginning of any sense of history. And for me, as for David Atwell, those Odeon interiors, even the less successful ones, 'seem to evoke nostalgically the very essence of the Odeon era'.

I am two years younger than the Odeon, Redhill. I belong to that generation weaned with Disney's *Bambi*. Our childhood notion of the supremely desirable career was 'to be a film star'. In the year of my birth, 1940, there were some 5500 cinemas in Britain. Today about 1100 remain. This is worse than 'decimation'. Time and again, David Atwell has to break off from the task of celebrating the cinemas' glories (a task which no one in the world is so well qualified to perform) to record another desecration, demolition, or threat. His book may do something to halt the massacre. Both text and pictures are eloquent arguments for giving statutory listing to the finest examples not yet so protected.

But this marvellous book is far more than a fighting manifesto. It is the most comprehensive and scholarly account yet written of cinema architecture in Britain. David Atwell is no indiscriminate apologist for everything that has happened in British cinema architecture. But his taste is splendidly catholic. He is sympathetic both to the Modern Movement and to the 'atmospheric' school which first appeared in Britain in 1929 – a post-Depression birth, one might say. It was perhaps only natural that as we were taking American films we should take the American-style cinemas to go with them: one would not present fancy chocolates in a shoe box. Lack of interest among our architects in what was happening on the Continent may have been no bad thing, whatever the sardonic P. Morton Shand thought. Instead of becoming mimic Mendelsohns and pastiche Poelzigs, British architects fell back on the congenial traditions of theatre architecture, with its bravura and extravagance, and fairground architecture (the 'showman's booth' derided by Shand) as well as composing their own variations on the American 'atmospherics'.

The survival of their buildings, *where* they survive – buildings people loved and could escape into from a world harsher than our own – is a flaunting rebuke to most contemporary architects with their bald, boring façades. Perhaps that, along with a measure of intelligent self-interest, is why architects have seldom been prominent among the champions of cinema architecture. There have been honourable exceptions: it was the great Goodhart-Rendel, in a *RIBA Journal* obituary of Thomas Verity (1937), who said of his 'sumptuous cinemas' that they were 'examples of such high architectural accomplishment that anyone is to be pitied who cannot enjoy them for their own sake'. Let the same strictures apply to anyone who is left unmoved by this book.

# PREFACE

No more pitiful degradation of an art has ever been presented than the prostitution of architecture that goes on daily in the construction of these huge buildings.

THOMAS E. TALLMADGE in 'Motion Picture News', 1928

N 1900 there was not a single building specifically built for use as a cinema. Less than 40 years later every major town had at least one picture palace, a total of some 5500 cinemas nationally. The cinema can thus be said, with good reason, to be the most important new building type of the 20th century. And yet for the most part cinema buildings have been reviled by architectural critics, and frequently by architects themselves. Little has been written about cinemas at any time, least of all in recent years, other than Dennis Sharp's excellent book *The Picture Palace*, which appeared in 1969. There is an almost total lack of available research on the subject. Here and there one encounters an enthusiastic local librarian or a student's dissertation but, for the most part, what has gone into this book is the result of original research and exploration.

Offering value judgments on the merits of cinema buildings is a delicate task especially so close to the present day in terms of architectural history, where many of the designers and protagonists concerned are still alive. It becomes especially invidious when comparing the relative qualities of the cinemas of one architect as opposed to another. However, opinions vary so widely on the merits of cinema buildings, from the outright antagonism of the Modern Movement architects of the thirties, to the perhaps over-indulgent and uncritically nostalgic eye of some present-day preservationists. My own view stands somewhere in between: a wholehearted admirer of the purely functional qualities of their design and the fantasy character of many of the interiors, but no dewy-eyed sentimentalist when considering their value, or should one say intrusion, in townscape terms. The external architectural contribution of the cinema was seldom high, and all too often they proved something of a disaster in the townscape, particularly when related to the urban scale of a shopping street. At the same time if the exteriors were a little short on architectural invention, many of the interiors were, and still are, masterpieces of inspired imaginative design. In my view the chief contribution of the cinemas were not the 'atmospheric' interiors which were exceeded in elaboration in other countries, but in the extensive use of artdeco interiors, and also the classic detailing of some more conventional auditoria. Both Odeons and Granadas stand apart from the remainder and are unique in terms of the history of cinema design elsewhere. The costs of building cinemas were high in relation to their short life expectancy, but the movie demanded a new kind of building, and in the 'super' cinema as it developed in the late twenties and thirties, I believe a worthy model was provided, capable of favourable comparison on its own terms with any theatre. Similarly, splendid though the greatest cinemas are that survive overseas, such as one or two of the American atmospherics, or the Tuschinski in Amsterdam, or the State in Sydney, the finest British examples of the Tooting Granada and the New Victoria can safely withstand that competition. It was with perfect justification that the Brixton Astoria was described as 'An Acre of Seats in a Garden of Dreams' at its opening.

My own reason for writing this book is perhaps best explained by the fact that in my youthful days of cinema-going in the fifties I was apt to be more interested in the decorations of the auditorium than I was in the activities on the screen. My upbringing was in an area near London where some of the finest super cinemas in the country were easily accessible.

The Chinese pagodas in Southall, the Spanish City in Ealing, and the Venetian extravagances of Tooting were all well loved by the time I was a teenager. Strong views held about the merits and demerits of particular cinemas were nurtured during an architectural training and fired by Dennis Sharp's pioneering book, to which anyone who writes about cinema buildings a decade later owes a great debt. My own researches have almost exactly filled the last decade, taking me to over a thousand cinemas in an ever-changing climate of accelerating closures, conversions to bingo, and twinning and tripling exercises. During this time I have seen more tantalising highlights from films of every description than I would have believed possible as I waited for house lights to come up, and inadvertently acquired more knowledge of the skills of bingo than must be good for anyone.

During all this time I have of course benefited enormously from the help and encouragement of my sometimes incredulous colleagues at the Greater London Council. In particular may I thank Louis Bondy and William Bell, successive Chairmen of the GLC Historic Buildings Committee, who have always viewed my efforts to preserve cinemas with support and interest, and even, I dare to hope, sometimes with sympathy. Also without the support of Ashley Barker, Surveyor of Historic Buildings to the GLC, this book might never have assumed the form it has, especially when I was asked in 1972 by the Department of the Environment to advise their Historic Buildings Council on which cinemas in London to preserve. I am pleased to say it was largely my efforts on that occasion that led to the statutory listing of the first nine cinemas in London, an act for which I am still more often blamed than congratulated!

Within the GLC Historic Buildings Division, I would like to pay special tribute to Anne Riches for her researches into Frank Verity; to Kenneth Mills, ever a mine of information on the most unexpected architects, and to Susan Beattie, Michael Kilburn, Martin Andrew, Martin O'Rourke and Peter Smith. A special word of thanks also to the GLC Photographic Unit and their head, Roy Ferriman, for producing so many excellent pictures used in this book, and in particular to Alan Turner, who laboured often photographing the interiors of cinemas, frequently under conditions of extreme difficulty. Several of these people have now moved on elsewhere to other tasks, and I can only hope these words of appreciation will find them.

Away from the GLC, people all over the country have helped me over the years in discovering cinemas and their history, and in acknowledging the particular assistance of as many as possible now, I must inevitably apologise to all those who have contributed and who have been omitted. Among the many reference libraries I have visited, the staff at Sheffield local history library were especially helpful, and an individual word of thanks to Mr J. Lilley at Chesterfield library. Mr G. L. M. Goodfellow provided much valuable information on Scottish theatres and cinemas; and also in Scotland an admirable dissertation on the cinemas of Dundee by Craig Ross Downie of the University of Dundee has proved of interest and assistance. Gillian Darley has tirelessly followed up leads for me in America; Victor Glasstone, David Cheshire and Christopher Brereton were all of assistance in assembling information about theatres that became cinemas. Particularly valuable help has come from Celia Clark,

Secretary of the Portsmouth Society, someone who has enough knowledge, enthusiasm and energy for six others. Ken Powell helped me with Manchester cinemas and Andrew Richardson with Liverpool. John Cannon of the Eastern Arts Association and Elizabeth Grice have both been of great assistance with their knowledge of East Anglia. Graham King discovered a splendid cache of rare cinema drawings for me deep in the plan store of Bromley Borough Council; and Gordon Miller and Winifred Cooper have been instrumental in drawing attention to the unique survival of the Electric Palace in Harwich, and its subsequent restoration. Over the years I have received help and a good deal of knowledge from Marcus Eavis and Richard Gray, respectively Secretary and Archivist of the Cinema Theatre Association. Among architects I have met, or who have taken the trouble to contact me may I particularly thank Leslie Kemp, formerly of Kemp and Tasker, E. Wamsley Lewis, designer of the New Victoria, and Robert Bullivant and Cecil Clavering. The last two named are of course the great link with the Odeon style and in this connection may I acknowledge my enormous debt to Allen Eyles, who knows more about the history of the Odeons than anyone else. Among cinema promoters, I must of course thank Rank Leisure Services (especially Chris Moore), EMI and Granada for affording me courtesy and access to their buildings at every turn of a very long road.

Finally, on a more personal note, may I thank my wife for her patience in the face of adversity, and Catherine Griffiths for the thankless task of elucidating sense from my manuscripts and typing them.

Any book that tries to extend available printed knowledge in the relatively uncharted waters, and against the surprisingly contradictory facts of cinema building research is necessarily subjective in matters of architectural opinion. Moreover errors of detail or fact are bound to have crept in, and all I can do is to crave indulgence in a massive task, and invite corrections where they are needed. It should be explained that the uses of all the cinemas I describe are as I found them at the time of inspection. They have been updated where necessary to July 1981, but *aficionados* of the cinema will not need reminding that uses can change with remarkable rapidity and regularity. Ten years ago the idea of preserving cinemas as historic buildings would have been dismissed by most people as an eccentric dream. Today, although cinema closures have been sadly insensitive with regard to their architectural merits, thirty-seven cinemas are protected by Government listing. Eventually I believe the finest of the super cinemas will be valued as highly as we now regard our Victorian public buildings or Edwardian theatres. I hope this book will be appreciated as a small contribution to the cause of saving a few more of these cinemas as permanent memorials to a vanished era.

David Atwell
July 1981

# 1

# THE AGE OF THE PENNY GAFF

The Cinema does not only cater for imbeciles, it breeds them. The commercial cinema is an entertainment for illiterate slaves.

THEODORE KOMISARJEVSKY

COMPARED WITH THE LIVE THEATRE the cinema, whether art form, industry or building, has had an astonishingly short life. As recently as 1900 there was not a single building specifically built for use as a cinema, and it was only in the last decade of the 19th century that the commercial potential was realised of film as an entertainment medium. Before embarking on the tale of how rival inventors in America, Britain, France and Germany more or less emerged together with their projectors in the mid-1890s, it is necessary to look briefly at what had happened earlier.

The origins of the idea of moving pictures on a screen are to be found in the innovations of the panorama and diorama, the forerunners of today's cinemas, but even before this, came the magic lantern. This has to do with the science of optics and the fascination exerted on the general public by illusionistic effects. The magic lantern was a 17th-century invention, and it was this, in an improved form, that introduced the paying public to the phenomenon of projected pictures. The earliest well-documented use of this perfected magic lantern was by Etienne Gaspard Robertson in Paris at the turn of the 18th century. The images were projected onto a calico screen from behind, and the eerie effects he produced apparently terrified his audience. What is even more interesting from the architectural point of view is that Robertson's exhibition room was evidently not dissimilar to the earliest cinema auditoria of the 1900s. It is described in F. Marion's *The Wonders of Optics* (London 1868): 'He used a room some sixty or eighty feet long, and twenty-four wide, which he hung entirely with black. Of this a strip twenty-five feet long was cut off and devoted to the manipulation of the phantasmagora. This portion of the apartment was separated from the spectators by a white calico screen, tightly strained from side to side, and at first concealed from view by a black curtain. The calico screen, which was about twenty feet square, was well soaked in a mixture of starch and fine gum arabic, in order to render it semi-transparent. The floor was raised about four or five feet at one end in order that the whole of the spectators might have a free and uninterrupted view of what was going on'. It is a tribute to the ingenuity of Robertson that he could make a box housing a lamp and two convex lenses create such startling illusions when moved backwards and forwards, or by changing the size of the aperture.

The idea of a panorama originated with the German painter Breizig, and was developed by a Scottish artist and inventor, Robert Barker, who exhibited in 1788 a series of paintings depicting a continuous view of Edinburgh from Carlton Hill. Basically the pictures were on curved surfaces forming a circle and the audience viewed them from a central point. It was a success, and Barker came to London where he opened a purpose-built building just off Leicester Square in 1793. The form of the Panorama can still be recognised in the structure of its successor, the French Catholic Church of Notre Dame de France in Leicester Place. Although the Panorama remained open for some 70 years, the technique was soon superseded by the Diorama. This was really an advanced type of panorama, with the paintings supplemented by changing scenic effects produced by moving magic lanterns and translucent colours. It was the invention of the celebrated Frenchman Louis Daguerre, and he opened his first Diorama in the Rue Sanson, Paris, in 1822. Here the audience revolved around within the giant cylinder lined with pictorial views, and watched the scenes through an aperture in the inner auditorium wall shaped like a proscenium opening.

Daguerre came to London immediately after his success in Paris and established the famous Diorama in Park Square East, Regent's Park, in 1823. The great rotunda was designed by Augustus Charles Pugin and was sited behind the centre of John Nash's stucco terrace, being reached through the middle house, which acted as the main foyer. As with the Panorama, the shell of the building is still recognisable, and considerable remains of the mechanical arrangements have been traced in spite of the fire which destroyed the Diorama in 1839; they are surrounded by much later rebuilding and conversion.

Another celebrated Diorama was the one built in the middle of Leicester Square in 1851. Wylde's Great Globe, as it was called, only lasted for ten years through a legal entanglement concerned with building on a public open space. An equally famous London home of animated photographs was the Egyptian Hall in Piccadilly, erected in 1812, with a curious front derived from Karnak, and designed by P. F. Robinson. The Egyptian style had a brief fashion or revival in the early 19th century, and a near twin to this building survives in Chapel Street, Penzance, Cornwall. The hall or auditorium in Piccadilly was similar in form to the early music halls, with a raked stalls area and a gallery carried on columns. The hall was to see the arrival of the cinematograph before its closure in 1905. It duly disappeared without trace.

Thomas Alva Edison invented his first Kinetoscope in 1891, having combined in 1889 with George Eastman to perfect frame-lined celluloid film. This was simply a peep-hole machine operated by a nickel in the slot, and the members of the paying public saw a continuous reel of film some fifteen metres long. It was not until May 1894 that the first 'peep-show' parlour opened in Chicago, and the first displays in England of Edison's invention were in the autumn of 1894 when ten peep-show instruments were installed at No 70 Oxford Street. The peep-show took the form of one person at a time viewing the endless band of 35mm film which moved continuously over a series of rollers. About 40 different films were available, each lasting about a minute. The new phenomenon attracted a great deal of attention and soon generated attempts by inventors all over Europe and America to turn the peep-show machine into projection apparatus. In November 1895 the Skladanowski brothers demonstrated their 'intermittent photographs' on a Bioscope, or double projector, in the Wintergarten, Berlin. In the following month, on 28 December 1895, the Lumière brothers gave the first public performance of their moving pictures in a café on the Boulevard des Capucines in Paris, and that is where the story really begins. In London, the first documented English projection of moving pictures took place on 14 January 1896 at the Royal Photographic Society, presented by Birt Acres, one of the Fellows.

These early displays were such a success with the public that the Lumière brothers patented their equipment, and they called it 'Cinématographie', the word which has remained in use until the present day. The first London demonstration of the new apparatus was on 20 February 1896 in the Marlborough Hall of the Royal Polytechnic Institute in Upper Regent Street, better known today as the Regent Street

Two early cinemas in Hackney photographed in 1914. The one on the right seems to be doing decidedly better business than the other

Polytechnic. In March, Robert Paul introduced his own invention, the 'Theatrograph' to a paying public at Olympia. Then, as recounted in chapter 2, these shows transferred on a more regular basis to existing theatres, the Empire and the Alhambra, both in Leicester Square. On 23 November 1896 Queen Victoria had a private showing at Windsor Castle of films made by the Lumière brothers, and this added respectability guaranteed the success of the new medium.

At the same time all this was happening in London, Edison was perfecting his own inventions in New York, and on 4 April 1896 the first display was given of 'Mr Edison's latest invention', the Vitascope. This new apparatus projected his continuous kinetoscope bands of film onto a large canvas screen, and on 23 April it was given the first public paying demonstration as part of a bigger variety programme. In 1897 Thomas L. Tally opened the first picture parlour in Los Angeles, but it was not exclusively devoted to moving pictures. Then in 1902 he opened his first 'Electric Theatre' in Los Angeles, the debut of the cinema building as a purpose-built and permanent form of public entertainment. These early cinema parlours in America, called Nickelodeons, were simply rectangular rooms with a small stage and screen at one end, and were named after their admission fees. Within two years there were several hundred and in 1903 came the first feature length film: 'The Great Train Robbery'.

In precisely the same way, the earliest British cinemas were called 'penny gaffs', and they began to present programmes of single-reeler films. What presents one of the most intriguing areas of investigation is identifying with any certainty which was the earliest purpose-built cinema, as opposed to a conversion of an existing hall or shop, and also which was devoted exclusively to the presentation of films. Regular nightly shows of films to fee-paying audiences were a common occurrence by the turn of the century, and many existing public halls were pressed into use to meet the new demand, such as the vast West End hall in Birmingham (long ago demolished). In these early days even railway arches in London were used for film shows. In *The Picture Palace*, Dennis Sharp claims the earliest building designed exclusively and especially for film shows was probably the Central Hall, Colne, Lancashire built for Joshua Duckworth in 1907, but long disused. However, for some years now, it has been accepted that the earliest purpose-built cinema was in London, the much altered, but still used, Bioscope (now the Biograph), a few doors away from the New Victoria cinema in Wilton Road, Victoria. This was opened in March 1905 by an American promoter, George Washington Grant, who built a new hall behind an existing row of shops, and converted one of them into the entrance foyer. The Biograph is certainly the earliest purpose-built cinema in London, but it has been so mutilated and modernised that its architectural interest is now largely academic. Indeed the original hall was re-opened after alteration as early as 24 May 1909. A. C. Bromhead opened his 'Daily Bioscope' in Bishopsgate Street, London on 23 May 1906, a conversion of existing premises.

Recent researches by the author have now revealed the existence of at least three cinemas of earlier date, one of which sadly closed as recently as 1977 to make way for redevelopment. This was the Haven in Stourport on Severn, Worcestershire, which was built as the Electric Theatre in 1904 on the site of an old tannery. Again this was a much altered building with very little original detail visible either outside or in the 368 seat auditorium. However, what is just as unusual and rare about this building is that it is quite well documented and, most infrequently for an early cinema, the name of the architects is known. They were Pritchard and Pritchard of Kidderminster (who also designed the Regal at Tenbury Wells), the builder was one Thomas Vale, and the cost of construction was £1300. It was a rectangular hall some 60 ft by 40 ft, originally seating about 300, and remained unaltered until 1933 when a balcony was added, increasing the seating capacity to 550. There had also been more recent changes.

It should also be mentioned within the context of these earlier cinema attributions that *The Builder* obituary on W. A. Dew, LRIBA on 7 September 1956 records that he designed a picture hall at Hyde, Cheshire in 1900. This is feasible, though unlikely, and it is not now possible to trace the building. In the absence of further evidence, this claim must be regarded as apocryphal. Just as early seem to have been two halls in Portsmouth, both regrettably now demolished. One was the Portland Hall in Kent Road which opened in 1901 and showed films nightly at admission prices ranging from 6d to 3/–. It had 800 seats, but had closed by the end of 1920. The other was the Victoria cinema in Commercial Road, which opened early in 1901 with 'Edison's Animated Pictures'

A well-preserved early cinema
in Portsmouth: the
Shaftesbury, opened in 1910
and now used for bingo

nightly at 8 pm, with matinées on Wednesdays and Saturdays. There was
also a 'full orchestral band'. In December 1901 top of the bill was *Wests Our
Navy* and four 2/6d family tickets could be purchased for 8/–. The cinema
closed in the fifties with *Expresso Bongo*, and the site is now occupied by
offices. It is interesting to note how relatively expensive were these early
admission prices.

As befits a busy port, Portsmouth and Southsea had a plethora of
early cinemas, 24 being licensed before the First World War, including
three non-permanent movable fairground enclosures. The Paragon Picture Palace in Lake Road advertised itself as late as the 1920s as having the
cheapest show in Portsmouth: admission was only 3d. No doubt a roaring
success with the sailors on shore leave. The most important early survival
in Portsmouth is the Shaftesbury (later Tatler) cinema in Kingston Road, a
730 seat auditorium opened on 14 May 1910, and still in use as a bingo
hall. The attractive front is virtually unchanged, although the interior has
been substantially altered and modernised over the years and until 1979

The almost untouched original auditorium of the Electric, Portobello Road, opened in 1905 and still used as a cinema

showed double bills of the *Clockwork Nympho* plus *Sexy Stewardesses* variety.

Where there seems little doubt is in the identity of the earliest unaltered cinema interior in Britain. This is the Electric in Portobello Road, a listed building in London's North Kensington area, built a few months after the Biograph in 1905, and known for a while as the Imperial before reverting to its original name. Although the exterior has been mutilated and is now faced in faience tiling, the scruffy interior, incredibly, survives almost entirely untouched and still in use. Like almost every early cinema, it is a simple rectangular hall with a barrel-vaulted roof, and moulded plasterwork arranged as ribs and as decorative panels. Occasionally, in these early interiors, there would be a small gallery or balcony across one end, although these were not usually added until the advent of the talkies, and similarly screens were simply on the end wall until sound necessitated the construction and bringing forward of proscenium arches to facilitate the installation of loudspeakers. The nature of the plaster ornament in these early halls was directly derived from that employed in contemporary Edwardian theatres and music halls. Some of these halls were more primitive still, highly decorative fronts with corrugated-iron sheds behind them. In the West End of London, as early as 1905, American Bioscope shows were Top of the Bill (item 13 on the programme), at

Detail of plasterwork in the
Electric, Portobello Road. The
theatrical tradition carries on

the London Coliseum. However, the early purpose-built cinemas were not built in great numbers before the Cinematograph Act, 1909, which became operative on 1 January 1910, and up until then existing halls on hire or conversions generally sufficed.

Another very early cinema that survives in mutilated form is the Coliseum in Brampton, Derbyshire. This opened in October 1907 as the Central Hall, but was exclusively devoted to films. Built by Charles Senior out of a disused chapel, it is recorded that on occasions (perhaps when she could not be persuaded otherwise), Mrs Senior would provide the entertainment between the single-reelers by climbing onto the stage, and obliging with such classic violin solos as 'The Gladiator's Farewell'. In 1939 the Coliseum suffered a serious fire, but was reconstructed and its seating increased from 420 to 609. It fell into disuse in 1952 and later became a paint warehouse. In late 1979 it was about to be further converted into a car sales showroom.

Two other very early cinemas of 1908 survive on the seaside front at Great Yarmouth, Norfolk. One is the Windmill, the other, originally

The Dara in Delancey Street, Camden Town. It assumed its present appearance in 1908 after use both as a public hall and a roller-skating rink

named the Palace of Light, had 1000 light bulbs on its front and it was built for C. B. Cochran (and is now statutorily listed for this reason). After improvements in 1910 to comply with the 1909 Cinematograph Act, it was renamed the Gem.

The year 1903 had seen a great national craze for roller skating and a large number of rinks were built, or again converted from existing public halls. Roller skating had first been popular in the eighties, but the 1903 craze, and a further revival in the years 1908–10 led to many rinks being opened in London by an American named C. B. Crawford. The typical entrance fee was 6d, and there were usually three sessions daily in the morning, afternoon and evening. Like skateboarding in the late seventies, it was a shortlived craze, and a substantial number of these buildings became early cinemas. There are two well-known examples in London. The more interesting is the Dara (now a bingo hall), in Delancey Street, Camden Town. This was built as a public hall in the 1880s, then became a skating rink in 1903, and finally was reconstructed as a cinema in 1908. It was at this date that the interesting pedimented entrance and the stuccoed flank wall to the street were formed, and although the interior is fairly plain, a rare survival is the original paybox. The Dara is maintained in good condition, and is a building that deserves government listing. The other is the Walpole Picture Theatre in Bond Street, Ealing, where the

The original pay-box of the Dara, Camden Town

Elevation of a proposed new cinema in Green Lane, Penge, dated 1909. The cinema was never built

skating rink was given a spanking new faience front in 1912, liberally ornamented with swags of foliage. After a long standing threat of redevelopment, the Walpole was closed for most of the seventies, but has enjoyed a brief spell recently as a carpet shop. It was demolished in 1981, but its facade is to be incorporated in the new development.

The 1909 Cinematograph Act was rendered necessary because of the inflammable cellulose-nitrate base with which films were manufactured. This readily enabled them to ignite or burst into flames with a positively explosive force. Cinema blazes had consequently become a well-publicised and regular happening and storage of films especially in damp or unsatisfactory conditions had become a hazardous operation. The main effect of the Act was to insist upon the provision of a separate fire-resistant projection box, and also upon the availability of fire-fighting appliances, such as buckets of dry sand, within the auditorium itself. Cinema owners had to spend more on their buildings and upon improving them, and the protection of the new Act proved to be an incentive to erect many more new purpose-built cinemas that could be advertised as complying with the new regulations.

They had new and ever more exotic names such as the Bijou, Gem, Coronet, Jewel, Imperial, Pictorium or Picturedrome. One of the first was a proposed electric theatre to be called the Cinematographé in Green Lane, Penge, south-east London. The original architect's drawings by Alfred Parnacott survive, dated April 1909, and indicate that the only way the unfortunate projectionist could reach his booth was by a trap door in

the ceiling of the gentleman's lavatory. The drawings, though perhaps not the building, are of high quality and it is a pity that the cinema appears never to have been built. However, many hundreds of others were constructed, and a surprising number of them still survive, almost invariably altered, and sometimes almost unrecognisable, in other uses such as car showrooms, shops, warehouses or factories. At the same time many have been demolished in recent years, and their uneventful disappearance has all too often gone unrecorded. Nevertheless, an entertaining afternoon can still be spent in almost any provincial city or London suburb spotting these early electric theatres in their present disguises.

Pyke's Cinematograph Theatre on Brixton Hill. Opened in 1910, this photograph was taken in the late forties when it was known as the New Royalty. It survives surprisingly intact in use as a sports shop

Among well-known London examples, the Coronet in Brentford High Street, (1909) has been recently demolished, as has the Globe in Putney (1910). Pyke's Cinematograph Theatre of 1910 in Clapham Junction survived as Newbolton's furniture store until it was destroyed by fire in March 1979. This was a particularly sad loss, for in spite of large plate-glass shop windows, the interior was nearly intact, richly embellished with plaster cupids. Another Pyke's Cinematograph Theatre, later called the Clifton and the New Royalty, survived as a cinema on Brixton Hill from 1910 until 1957. It now does service as a sports shop, but the front is relatively little altered. The elaborate and little changed Cinema Royal in Chiswick High Road, near Turnham Green, is now a furniture shop; yet another, the Plaza, Colliers Wood is used as a garage showroom. The Ben Hur, Stepney of 1911 is still in use for bingo, so is another very early cinema in Deptford High Street, built behind a mid-Victorian building on the street frontage which had the ground floor converted into a foyer. The Curzon in Sutton, utterly mutilated, was built in 1911 and is still in use as Studios 1, 2 and 3. The Screen on Islington Green, now in use as an 'art' cinema, also dates from 1911, but has been unsympathetically altered in recent years. Another example in use is the Imperial in Clapham Junction, renamed the Ruby in 1973. This began life as a concert

A unique photograph taken
on 27 April 1911 of Albury
Street, Deptford. At the end,
in Deptford High Street, is the
Electric Palace, still in use
today as a bingo hall

The Coliseum, Harlesden,
London. An incredibly
claustrophobic interior of 1912
still used as a cinema

hall in 1890 and drifted into use as a music hall in 1894. Films were already being shown by 1910, and it was finally converted into its present form as a cinema in 1914. Also in use and in excellent condition is the Coliseum in Harlesden. The front was altered about 1930, but the amusingly claustrophobic little auditorium with a tiny balcony has hardly changed at all since 1912. Perhaps the grandest of all surviving early cinemas is the Parkhurst in Holloway Road, designed to seat 560, and which opened on 10 April 1908. Virtually untouched, it is now the North London Polytechnic theatre. The architect's drawings and specifications also survive, dated 1913, for a proposed cinematograph theatre to be called the Orpheum in High Street, Chislehurst. Prepared by H. W. Idle, the front, converted from an existing shop, was to display some earnest entreaties about the nature of the films to be shown. One panel proclaimed that 'Our pictures are instructive and amusing without vulgarity', and another 'All the latest pictures – the world before your eyes'. One assumes the local burghers of Chislehurst were well satisfied with the proposed moral tone of their latest electric theatre. Incidentally, the hall behind was to be 70 ft long and only 11 ft wide, 28 rows each of six seats with a three feet wide side passage. Some other examples of early cinemas that can be recognised around the suburbs are in Station Road, Hampton (used as offices), the Metro cinema in High Street, Willesden (almost hidden behind hoardings); and the forlorn fragments of a once elaborate building in Lewis Road, Richmond, designed in 1910 by Brewer, Smith and Brewer; the so-called 'Clutch Centre' in New Cross; and the Electric Pavilion in Brixton (1911), now the Ritzy.

These early cinemas cannot be said to possess any particular architectural merit, and they were mostly plain halls with an ornate façade, derived from fairground presentation, simply stuck on the front. However, as the taste and appetite for cinemas grew, so did their degree of

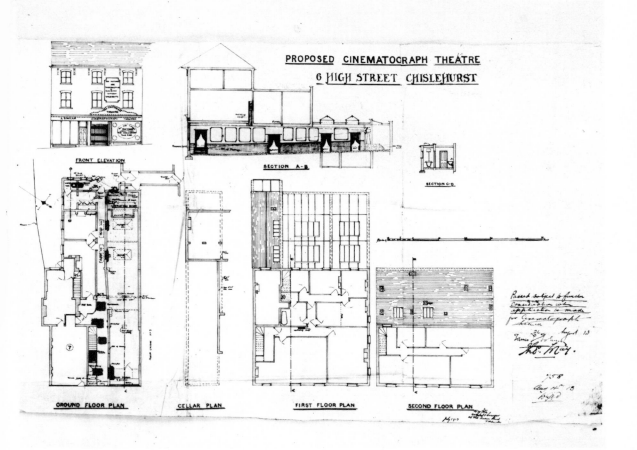

Drawings of the proposed Orpheum in Chislehurst, Kent, prepared in 1913. The panel declares 'Our pictures are instructive and amusing without vulgarity'. The hall was 70 ft long and only 11 ft wide!

The Walpole Picture Theatre in Ealing. An early design (1912) by J. Stanley Beard destined for early demolition

15

An early cinema in Brentford
High Street that was never
converted to sound. Due for
demolition for road widening
in 1981

A once fine early cinema in
Richmond designed in 1910 by
Brewer, Smith and Brewer.
Plans and elevations appear
on the facing page

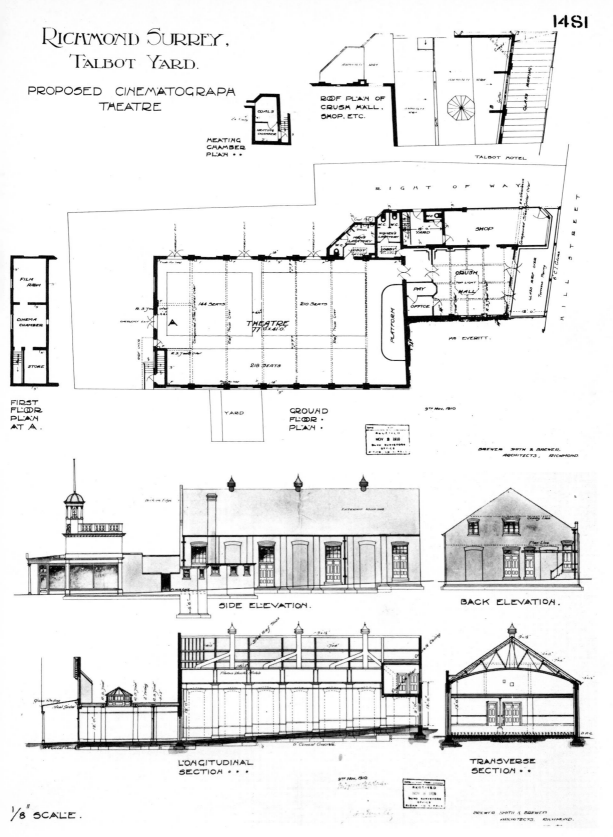

RICHMOND SURREY,
TALBOT YARD.

PROPOSED CINEMATOGRAPH
THEATRE

HEATING
CHAMBER
PLAN

ROOF PLAN OF
CRUSH MALL.
SHOP. ETC.

1481

TALBOT HOTEL

RIGHT OF WAY

SHOP

CRUSH
MALL

PAY
OFFICE

PLATFORM

THEATRE
77.0 x 41.0

144 Seats

210 Seats

218 Seats

FIRST
FLOOR
PLAN
AT A.

FILM
ROOM

CINEMA
CHAMBER

STORE

YARD

GROUND
FLOOR
PLAN

9TH NOV. 1910

Mr EVERITT.

BREWER SMITH & BREWER.
ARCHITECTS, RICHMOND

SIDE ELEVATION.

BACK ELEVATION.

LONGITUDINAL
SECTION

TRANSVERSE
SECTION

⅛" SCALE.

9TH NOV. 1910

BREWER SMITH & BREWER.
ARCHITECTS, RICHMOND.

One of the saddest losses among early cinemas: the Hackney Pavilion built in 1913 and demolished in 1972

elaboration, and several of the London cinemas built just before the First World War were very finely decorated and had sizeable balconies. Regrettably, the most splendid have now been demolished, like the former Odeon in Upper Street, Islington, the Astoria in Wastdale Road, Forest Hill, and the Hackney Pavilion (of 1913, demolished 1972), which had perhaps the finest interior of its date and type in Britain. Another tragic loss was the Ionic, Golders Green, built in 1912 and opened by the great ballerina Anna Pavlova, and needlessly demolished in 1972 to make way for a supermarket; if this cinema could have survived just a few more months it would undoubtedly have been listed. It was a perfect example of a classical 'pomp' front grafted onto a plain brick box-like hall, and the hall itself was unchanged, with an interesting serpentine shape to the balcony, and rows of tiny boxes along the sides evidently designed for privacy rather than any possibility of seeing more than one corner of the screen. Nevertheless there are survivors: the Maida Vale Picture House, later the Carlton, survives as a Mecca bingo club, and has a fine domed front façade. The Grange in Kilburn High Road was built in 1914 and today enjoys theatrical use. It has a domed corner entrance and a galleried foyer (with a particularly good thirties lantern light fitting), and a spacious 1300 seat auditorium that has been little altered apart from the apparent removal of applied fibrous plaster decoration from the balcony front. The Gaumont in Hill Street, Richmond was designed by Sydney W. Davis and opened on Christmas Eve 1914 as the Royalty Electric Theatre. Entered through an 18th-century redbrick town house, it is now a listed building. Little altered, it is now closed and threatened with redevelopment; subject of a public enquiry in June 1981

The superb auditorium of the
Hackney Pavilion, fully the
equal of any contemporary
Edwardian theatre

Detail of the plasterwork and
an ornamental box at the
Hackney Pavilion

The Ionic, Golders Green.
Built in 1912, it was
demolished in 1972. The front
was a perfect example of a
'show' façade stuck on a
functional brick box

The unusual and shapely
auditorium of the Ionic,
Golders Green. Note the rows
of boxes ensuring privacy but
poor visibility

The Maida Vale Picture
House, designed in 1912, and
still intact as a bingo hall

The attractive galleried foyer
of the Kilburn Grange,
opened in 1914. Note the
splended thirties light fitting

The Rialto in London's Coventry Street. A beautifully preserved interior of 1913, threatened with demolition. Designed by Hippolyte Blanc

In the West End of London three early cinemas survived until recent years. Now only one is left and that is destined for demolition. The two that have been already demolished to make way for redevelopment were in Tottenham Court Road; the Majestic Picturedrome (later the Continentale) of 1912, and only a few doors away, the Berkeley of the same year with a virtually identical auditorium. The survivor at the time of writing is the Rialto, Coventry Street. It was built in 1913 at a cost of £31,000 and was called the West End Theatre when first constructed, although no stage facilities were in fact provided. The architect was an exotically named Parisian, Hippolyte Blanc, and the interior decoration was designed by Horace Gilbert of Gilbert and Constanduros. The interior has remained intact to a most surprising degree considering its continuous use in the West End as a cinema for over 65 years. Small in size, seating just under 600 in stalls and circle, the cinema boasts exceptionally rich plasterwork. An impressive two-storey hall with double staircase leads to a vigorously ornamented yet intimate auditorium.

Another fascinating sideline in the design of these early cinemas is that it has not been appreciated until recently that the great theatre architect Frank Matcham was involved in the design of a number of cinemas both before and immediately after the war. The last of his cinema

The interior of the Electra Palace in Fitzalan Square, Sheffield (designed in 1912 by Hickton and Farmer) was in beautiful condition when this picture was taken in the 1960s. Within a few years every vestige of decorative plasterwork had been stripped out by Classic Cinemas

output to survive, the Broadway Cinema, Hammersmith of 1913 was demolished in 1979. However, Matcham's much later Super in Magdalen Street, Oxford, (1922–4) is of some interest.

In 1912 the *London Evening News* recorded that there were some 500 cinemas open in London and its suburbs, and that they had an average staff of eight. The *Kine Year Book* of 1913 records that in the north-west there were 111 cinemas in Manchester alone and 22 in Liverpool. The development of early cinemas had therefore continued apace in the provinces, if without the concentrations of such buildings to be found in London. But in the provincial cities, the early cinemas have suffered particularly grievously: in Manchester only nine of the 111 cinemas still retain worthwhile indications of their origins. Outstanding among these is the listed Grosvenor Picture Palace in Oxford Road. Dating from 1912 it is a most impressive corner building faced in white faience tiling with an effective corner dome. It had been closed as a cinema by mid-1979, although the original auditorium was still intact, and a billiard hall was operating in the basement. The Salford Cinema (later the Rex) is another little altered corner building of somewhat similar form, dated 1912, on a segmental pediment above the side entrance, and is now used for bingo. The Corona, Gorton is an altogether more ambitious building with an ostentatiously bold front façade dating also from 1912. Used now as the Mayflower Cabaret Club, the interior has been altered to its detriment in recent years.

The Corona, Gorton, Manchester. Dated 1912, this is a splendid survival from the early days when it is recorded that Manchester already had 111 cinemas in 1913

Liverpool has no early survivals of importance unless the act of God that recently converted the early Picture House of 1913 (that showed sex films) into the Shrine of the Blessed Sacrament can be counted as being of more than local significance. Sheffield has been almost as unlucky. In the last 15 years, twelve early cinemas have been demolished, including the fine Palace in Union Street (1910), and the Unity Picture Palace (1913) designed by Gibbs, Flockton and Teather. The Electra Palace in Fitzalan

The early Electra Palace in Eckington, Derbyshire (c 1912) approaching a seedy end in this photograph taken in 1966

Square, designed in 1912 by Hickton and Farmer, survives in a dismally mutilated form as the Classic cinema. The stone front, decorated with sculpted Egyptian heads, is entirely hidden by an overall advertising screen of typically 'Classic' insensitivity, and all the decorative plasterwork has been stripped away internally.

Blackburn has one very early survivor: the Alexandra Hall in Dock Street, which opened at Easter in 1909. Although still in use as a cinema, it is completely plain and of relatively little interest.

The solitary interesting survival in Oxford is the Penultimate Picture Palace in Jeune Street, which was designed by local architect John R. Wilkins, and opened on 25 February 1911. Closed by 1920 it became a furniture store until it re-opened as the Penultimate in July 1976. It has a typical early pedimented and stuccoed show front in its original condition, but the interior has been modernised. Hull retains one curious and listed early cinema called the Tower, but ornamented in fact with a pair of domes. It opened in 1914 and was designed in a debased art nouveau style by J. Percival Binks.

In Derbyshire, the Plaza, Bolsover, is a pre-first World War cinema used for bingo since 1966. It has an unusually subdued narrow street frontage in half-timbered style leading to a 'back to front' auditorium (ie entry from beside the screen). The interior was modernised in about 1930

The Electra, Rotherham (1911) shortly before demolition in 1972

with the coming of the talkies, when the circle and proscenium arch were added, and a series of art deco motifs applied to the side walls. The present manager remembers, as a boy in the early 1920s, the '2d rush' on Saturday afternoons for the back stalls. He would then sit below the beam of light armed with a pea shooter and fire his ammunition up into it until the show was brought to a halt.

One of the most publicised of the frequent early cinema fires occurred in Chesterfield at the Picture Palace in Burlington Street, a cinema that had opened in September 1910. The fire broke out on 27 December 1911, and proved a tragic indictment on the ingenuity of the manager who had devised the idea of having local children to entertain the patrons from the stage between the films. Thirty children were being used on this occasion for an 'Eskimo scene', and the dress of one of them caught fire in the dressing room. In the following inferno five children died, and not unexpectedly the Picture Palace closed for ever.

The small market town of Beverley retains a remarkable survival in the form of the Picture Playhouse. Not a purpose-built cinema, it began life in 1886 as the Corn Exchange, and was converted to a full-time cinema in 1910 by Ernest Symmons, whose wife continued to run the cinema after his death and established a record of family continuity with the cinema stretching over 65 years. The picturesque baroque redbrick

Auditorium of the Picture
Playhouse, Beverley, showing
the curious form of the gallery

exterior is that of the old Corn Exchange of 1886, and the interior has
changed little since 1910 with a small gallery of unusually shapely design.
A 1910 programme for the Picture Playhouse advertised two shows
nightly: 'A great show, one drama lasting over ten minutes . . . tonight
four of the most exciting dramas including a thrilling Western cowboy . . .
five short comics, interest and trick films'. On 1 June 1914 the programme
of films declared:

> Work in the morning
> Pictures at night
> Braces the system
> And keeps the heart light.

Ernest Symmons himself made numerous films in and around Beverley
for the Picture Playhouse, and for many years claimed he ran the only
cinema in the country that regularly produced its own newsreel. The
Playhouse remained a full-time cinema until 1962, when Mrs Symmons
reluctantly went over to bingo; however, films returned on a part-time
basis in 1972. As late as 1958, the monthly film programme for the
Playhouse announced: 'Time passes and Life is brief. Enjoy the fleeting
moments to the full, spend the evening at the little Picture House and
bring your friends with you. A short walk, a comfortable seat, a Good
Programme, a little talk over things in a congenial atmosphere will send
you home with that HAPPY feeling of having spent the evening well'.
They were sentiments that could have equally well have applied to the
intentions of any of the early cinema operators.

Two early cinemas of especial interest survive in East Anglia. The
Gainsborough cinema in Sudbury became a listed building in November
1973. Situated in an area always noted for a keen interest in cinema (the
first displays of moving pictures took place in Bury St Edmunds as early
as 1898), this building was designed by Sidney Naish, and constructed by

The Electric Palace, Harwich looking prosperous soon after it opened in 1911

the local firm of Grimwood for about £600. An interesting feature was the extensive use of reinforced concrete walls. The Gainsborough opened on 15 July 1912, and seated about 600, including a small balcony. The exterior, a little lumpish in proportion, and the restrained decoration of the interior remain little altered today in a cinema which is still in full-time use.

The rarest and most precious survival in all England has been left almost until last: the Electric Palace in Harwich. It was not opened until 29 November 1911, so it is not by any means one of the earliest cinemas. What sets it aside from all others is not only its architectural elegance and gentle good humour, but also its miraculously unaltered state. It was designed by the Ipswich architect Harold Ridley Hooper, whose original drawings survive, and was an early commission for a young architect aged 26 years. It came from Charles Thurston, head of East Anglia's most celebrated family of travelling fairground showmen. The social history of the Electric Palace is very fully recorded. The first night programme consisted of *The Battle of Trafalgar and the Death of Nelson*; a thrilling prairie story called *The Cowboy's Devotedness*; *Harry the Footballer*, and a number of short supporting comedies accompanied by a pianist in the pit. Incidentally, usherettes were paid 5/- per week at the Palace. On 11 May 1912 the Electric Palace was able to boast in its weekly newspaper advertisement 'Always a good up-to-date programme, Superb ventilation, strictly Sedate and Orderly', and on 29 June the same year the cinema had become 'Cosy, Cool, and Convenient'. Other programmes of this period included such evocatively titled epics as *Wiffles as Hero, A Pair of Trousers, The Sailor's Love Letters, The Maid of the Pie-Faced Indians, The Acrobat's Joke* and *The Municipal Water Cart*! During the First World War, no doubt to help entertain the many sailors from the port, variety became an essential part of the film programmes. On one occasion the 'only lady mimic of instruments, animals and babies' was billed to appear; on another an illusionist called 'Pharoah the Egyptian'; another performer was Cliff Newman, a tenor who did a camp fire scene around the song 'You've been along gone for the wood'; and again there was a negro sand dancer (*sic*) who did his act on a table for fifteen minutes. No doubt every act was a winner!

Sound came on 10 March 1930 with Al Jolson's *The Singing Fool*, and the Palace staggered on in the face of fierce competition from a new super cinema nearby throughout the thirties and forties. It continued its decline and on 3 November 1956, the Palace closed after the last show, so suddenly that admission tickets were even left in the machines in the paybox. The cinema remained locked up, forgotten and mercifully free from any severe vandalism until discovered in June 1972 by Gordon Miller and a team of students from Kingston Polytechnic, who were conducting a town study of Harwich. The significance of their discovery was not lost upon the Department of the Environment, who listed the Palace in September the same year.

The Electric Palace, with a seating capacity of 308, is the epitome of the pre-First World War cinema. A slightly pompous and overscaled stucco front with a segmental pediment is stuck on a rectangular brick hall some 70 ft long and 30 ft wide. The front is frivolous, yet elegantly detailed and proportioned, and constructed exactly in the manner of a stage set. The

interior is simple with a barrel-vaulted ceiling and moulded plaster ribs
and panels, less elaborate but similar in concept to the Electric in London's Portobello Road. For the past few years, with government historic
buildings grant aid and contributed funds, an enthusiastic local team of
volunteers have been painstakingly restoring the Palace to something
approaching its original glory, under the aegis of an Electric Palace trust
with charitable status. Successfully reversing the seemingly irreversible
trends of long-term decay is both expensive and skilled, and it is to be
hoped that this pioneering effort on a remarkable cinema will serve as an
excellent example to other local cinema preservation societies.

Outside England, little remains to be described. In Wales, it is to
Swansea that one must turn for the only two buildings of national interest
or importance. The first is the Carlton cinema in Oxford Street, with a
magnificent front façade that has been the subject of a long preservation
battle since October 1977. The Carlton was designed in 1912 by Sir
Charles Tamlin Ruthen and opened on 18 January 1914. Ruthen was a
very prominent local architect and councillor who designed a number of
Swansea's public buildings and was also Britain's National Director of
Housing from 1924–6. The front is monumental, lively and theatrical in
its effect and proportion, and was called 'the most sumptuous picture
house in Wales' at its opening. Faced in white faience tiling, there are
energetic Doulton friezes of dancing cherubs, a pair of baroque domes,
and an enormous curved semi-domed glass window that formerly lit the
café/restaurant and palm court at balcony level. In contrast to all this
external flamboyance, the interior, which has been extensively modernised, is plain and of no special note. The other Swansea cinema is the
Castle, literally hiding alongside the medieval ruins, a small and little
altered cinema of 1911 with a dignified and well-proportioned stone
front.

The Carlton in Oxford Street, Swansea. A palatial cinema designed in 1912 by Sir Charles Tamlin Ruthen.

In Scotland few early cinemas of any interest have remained intact. The earliest shows of Edison's peep-show pictures were given in Edinburgh at Moss's Carnival in the Waverley Market on 24 December 1894, and moving pictures made their debut in a theatre (the Empire Palace, Edinburgh) on 13 April 1896. The first cinema opened in the centre of Glasgow in 1909. It was called the Electric Theatre, but it has now gone, as have almost all the Glasgow cinemas of importance. In Edinburgh, the Palace Picture Palace of 1911 in St Bernard's Row, Stockbridge appears to have been the earliest; it survives although closed; similarly the Haymarket cinema of 1912 in Dalry Road. There was a fine intact early cinema in Corstorphine until demolition in the early seventies. An interesting, slightly later survival in Glasgow is the Salon in Vinicombe Street, dated 1913. It has a beautiful pilastered interior with some excellent back-lit decorative stained glass.

Before concluding this chapter, a few words should be added about the tented 'non-permanent enclosure' bioscope shows that toured the fairgrounds of the country, until they were effectively ended by the fire precaution requirements of the 1909 Cinematograph Act. The travelling shows were on the move immediately after the first London displays of moving pictures early in 1896. In October the same year, Randall Williams had a Bioscope show at Hull Fair. In Nottingham the next year, the Goose Fair was the venue for two rival shows; Collin's Living Pictures and Captain T. Payne's Electric Bioscope. Admission to these shows was 2d for adults and 1d for children. The tented structures were on average about 60 ft by 40 ft in size and fronted by an elaborately carved and painted wooden front incorporating the paybox. They were garishly illuminated at night and frequently had a steam organ to add to the cacophony of noise that they, no doubt, already generated. There was always a strong element of competition between the various travelling Bioscope shows, not only in the matter of films, but mainly in the spectacular manner of their presentation with booths and dancing girls, and the decorative frontages to the tents. The best-known shows were run by the Collins family, and the same Thurston family of Harwich fame. However, the whole structures were of course extremely inflammable and a number of serious fires were recorded. As one of the effects of the 1909 Act the shows almost all disappeared during 1910, most of them having had a life of less than ten years, and their operators turned their attention to the building of more permanent cinemas in which to show their films.

Technically, by the years just before the First World War, films had improved out of all recognition from those early experiments. The use of colour by hand tinting the negatives was becoming very popular, and as early as 24 February 1913, the programme at the London Coliseum was advertising a film in *Kinemacolor*, 'Stereoscopic pictures in all the glorious colours of nature without hand colouring or machine tinting of any kind'.

At the outbreak of war in 1914 it was estimated that there were about 4500 of the early cinemas in operation. Unlike the Second World War, there was a slump in attendances during the four years until 1918, and by the time the war ended up to a quarter of the cinemas had closed for ever. Thus, the scene was set for a new era of constructing bigger and better cinemas amid the hopes and aspirations of the emergent twenties.

# 2

# FROM THEATRE TO CINEMA

Enter the dreamhouse, brothers and sisters, leaving
Your debts asleep, your history at the door:
This is the home for heroes, and this loving
Darkness a fur you can afford.

C. DAY LEWIS
from 'Newsreel'

ROM THE VERY EARLIEST DAYS of cinematograph performances, Britain's enormous legacy of late Victorian and Edwardian theatres and music halls was turned over to film shows. It had been in March 1896 that the first public demonstration of the Lumière brothers' patent equipment had taken place in London at the old Empire Music Hall in Leicester Square. And on 25 March 1896 Robert Paul began a two-week season at the Alhambra theatre in Leicester Square with his 'Animatograph', a display of the 'new pictures'. Thus two existing theatres, the Empire and the Alhambra, were the first places in England to display shows of the new animated pictures on a regular nightly basis to a fee-paying public. Finally from 9 November 1896, the Lumières' 'Cinématographie' became a permanent part of the variety shows at the Empire, Leicester Square.

The old Empire Music Hall had been originally designed in 1882 by Thomas Verity, opening on 17 April 1884, and it survived until 1925 when MGM's British distribution organisation Jury-Metro-Goldwyn acquired the ageing theatre for redevelopment as a new cinema. This was to be the only British work of the celebrated Scottish-born architect Thomas W. Lamb, who made his name in the United States with his famous cinemas of the 'hard top' school (ie in accordance with correct classical design practice: see chapter 4) for Loew's, MGM's parent company. At the Empire he collaborated with Frank Matcham's practice, who presumably

*On previous page* Frank Matcham's Borough Theatre of 1895 in Stratford, East London, partly rebuilt in 1930 as the Rex cinema

The original Empire Theatre, Leicester Square

The Empire as reconstructed by Thomas Lamb and Frank Matcham

carried out the day-to-day site supervision for him. Frank Matcham, perhaps the greatest theatre designer that Britain has produced, had died five years earlier in 1920, although his practice continues in his name to the present day. The rebuilt Empire, seating 3133, making it the biggest West End cinema, opened on 8 November 1928, and it was in every way a magnificent showplace with a front façade in rich Italian Renaissance style fully in line with Lamb's usual grandiose American manner. Inside there was an immense foyer with a double marble staircase, walnut-panelled walls with large mirrors, and crystal chandeliers hanging from an ornately moulded plaster ceiling. The auditorium owed much of its effect and planning to Matcham's earlier masterpiece, the London Palladium in Argyll Street, which was opened on 26 December 1910. The main feature, as in the Palladium, was the immense circle which extended over much of the stalls area and took up nearly half the theatre's seating capacity. Full stage facilities were provided and the Empire was styled 'The Showplace of the Nation', in all advertising matter. In spite of

Cinemascope, falling attendances during the fifties cruelly exposed the Empire's uneconomic size, and it finally closed on 28 May 1961 in order to be reconstructed a second time.

The architect retained for this scheme was none other than the great George Coles, of whom much will appear in chapters 5 and 7 about his work in the late twenties and thirties, but was here virtually coming out of retirement to produce his last major scheme before his death in 1963. Basically he split the old theatre horizontally into two, with a new Mecca ballroom in the old stalls area, and a new stadium-style cinema auditorium on the site of the circle. The new cinema seated 1336 and, compared to his earlier work, finds Coles in very restrained mood. It is grandly conceived, but the blandly tiled walls and ceiling with their modest changing coloured light sequences create little sense of occasion. However, one great success is the luxuriously sprung seating. Typical of the new breed of plain, utilitarian post-war cinemas, it fails to achieve real distinction through either its decorations or its modernity.

The Alhambra, Leicester Square about 1930

Astonishing Indian
decorations in Frank
Matcham's Olympia Theatre,
Liverpool, which opened in
1904 and became a cinema in
1925. It is now a bingo club

The Alhambra was visually one of the most striking theatres ever
built, its Moorish fantasies having originated in 1850 before the Great
Exhibition. It was to have been the Royal Panopticon of Science and Art, a
building of colossal Saracenic pretension, the like of which had never
before been seen in the capital. Its architect was T. Hayter Lewis. The
Panopticon eventually opened on 18 March 1854, and was a fairly spectacular failure as a place of 'artistic and scientific edification'. It was duly
sold and reopened on 3 April 1858 as the Alhambra Palace, with Howes
and Cushing's American circus. Its new owner E. T. Smith soon obtained
a licence for music and dancing, and in 1860 built a proscenium arch to
form a stage area, provided tables and chairs in the old circus arena, and
renamed the building the Royal Alhambra Palace Music Hall. On the
night of 7 September 1882, the whole theatre was gutted by fire. However

it was rebuilt completely in the old style, but this time using fireproof materials, and the Alhambra reopened again on 3 December 1883. Further major alterations followed in 1907 and 1912 to facilitate the mixed shows of films and variety that were the principal offerings, although the Alhambra, with its huge stage, enjoyed a high reputation as the favoured venue for visiting international ballet companies such as Diaghilev's *ballets russes*. It was finally converted to full-time cinema use in 1929 and eventually demolished in 1936 to make way for the equally distinctive all-black Odeon, Leicester Square. Although undeniably a somewhat faded and tatty relic by the time of its closure, the exoticism of the old Alhambra was a sad loss for London's West End, and the external severity of its replacement proved a rather humourless substitute.

It is arguable as to when the first theatre was converted to permanent cinematograph performances. It has been claimed on a number of occasions that this honour should go to the Theatre Royal, Attercliffe, Sheffield. This is based on a list of Sheffield cinemas with their opening dates compiled in 1931 by the local Social Survey Committee, which gives 1904 as the opening date for the Theatre Royal. However it is recorded elsewhere in local archives that this theatre (now demolished) was originally opened on 26 July 1897 (having been designed by Flockton, Gibbs and Flockton), and had vaudeville shows until at least 1907. It is fair therefore to assume, as had happened at a good many other theatres by this time, that film shows combined or alternating with music hall or

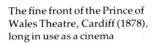

The fine front of the Prince of Wales Theatre, Cardiff (1878), long in use as a cinema

variety turns first became a feature at Attercliffe in 1904 and continued in this fashion for three years, and there seems no doubt that the Theatre Royal did become a full-time cinema during 1907. In spite of exhaustive researches, it has been impossible to establish that any other existing theatre or music hall was exclusively showing films before 1907.

A very interesting early conversion occurred in Portsmouth. This was Vento's Temple of Varieties on the corner of Leonard Street and Lake Road, built originally in the early 1880s by Henry Vento. In about 1885 it passed to Frank Pearce who proceeded to redecorate the theatre and renamed it the People's Palace, only to see it burned down on the day it was due to reopen. He completely rebuilt the theatre, and ran shows there until 1910. There is evidence that moving pictures were shown there as early as 1901 and certainly throughout Edwardian times admission, which could be gained for as little as 2d, gave patrons ten turns, including 'The People's Bioscope', acrobats, ventriloquists, vocalists, comedians and dramatic sketches. In January 1910 the People's Palace passed to W. Jury and became a full-time cinema as Jury's Picture House. In December 1914 the licence was transferred back to Frank Pearce, who renamed the building the Palladium cinema. It next received a completely new façade, entrance and enlarged front of house in 1921 designed by A. E. Cogswell, and survived until 15 November 1930, when it closed with the film *Atlantic*. It reopened intermittently during the thirties, but closed with the outbreak of war and lay derelict until the 1950s when it was converted to Bolloms Store. It later became Blundell's warehouse and, although mutilated, is still recognisable.

Portsmouth is absolutely typical of every provincial city in that all seven of its theatres did service as a cinema for some part of its life, and it is undoubtedly true that the majority of theatres enjoyed a degree of cinema use before 1939, particularly those in the suburbs of larger towns or cities. In 1979, out of 318 existing theatre buildings still identifiable in Britain, 43 were in use as cinemas. Occasionally one encounters examples of theatres that became cinemas and have recently made the transition back to theatres again, such as the Opera House, Buxton, the Palace Theatre, Newark and the Theatre Royal, Winchester, all of Edwardian date.

The earliest recorded full-time change of use from theatre to cinema in London is the Balham Empire in 1907. This had been designed as the Balham Empire Music Hall in 1900 by W. Hancock and was built on the site of former swimming baths. It seated 766 and was quite plain with simple wall pilasters and a single balcony with boxes. When converted into a cinema, it was renamed the Theatre de Luxe. It was always a hall on backland with a narrow high arched entrance set in an Edwardian shopping parade. It survived intact until recent years, but after closure, was eventually demolished in 1974.

Perhaps the most interesting long-term cinema use in London is the Coronet, Notting Hill Gate. Designed in 1898 by W. G. R. Sprague, this is the earliest complete theatre by an architect now regarded as being of comparable stature to Phipps and Matcham. Sprague's career spanned the world of theatre design from 1890 until in his last building, the Streatham Hill Theatre of 1929, we find him consciously adopting some of the clichés of contemporary cinema design. The Coronet is in his best

The Coronet Theatre, Notting Hill Gate (1898 by W. G. R. Sprague). A cinema since 1916

Interior of the Coronet showing where the boxes were removed in 1923

The Palaseum in London's East End. Opened as Fienman's Yiddish Theatre in 1912, it became a cinema within a few weeks

early classical 'French' style, with rich plaster decoration handled with a consistently light touch. In spite of a distinguished theatrical launching, which included the only appearance of Sarah Bernhardt and Mrs Patrick Campbell on stage together in the original French version of *Pelléas et Mélisande*, and the first appearance on any stage of Zena and Phyllis Dare in pantomime as the 'Babes in the Wood', the Coronet was never a great success and was already showing films by 1916. In 1923 the boxes were removed and the gallery withdrawn from use, and the theatre became a

The 1880s concert room in the Royal Agricultural Hall as converted in 1908 to the Blue Hall cinema

full-time cinema never to revert. After the war it was renamed the Gaumont, but has recently (1977) returned to its original name. Internally it is still in its appearance a little altered theatre and smells like one.

The Palaseum Theatre in Commercial Road in the heart of London's East End is a real curiosity. Designed in 1911 by George Billings, Wright and Company, it opened in March 1912 as Fienman's Yiddish Theatre with what has been rather mischievously described as the 'first . . . and last Jewish Opera'. Within weeks Fienman's had become the Palaseum, and has remained so ever since; it now shows Asian films. The small auditorium and stage are intact, though somewhat modernised, and the whole building, with its jokey Moorish façade, is fully in the manner of an early cinema.

The Islington Palace, in Upper Street, was built in 1861–2 as a large concert room, and is part of the Royal Agricultural Hall complex designed by Frederick Peck of Maidstone. In 1876 the Mohawk Minstrels took over the hall and in 1902 it was acquired by Gibbons as one of the first of his music halls. Cinema use came very early with conversion in 1908 as the Blue Hall cinema; later the side balconies were removed, and later still the cinema, by then a Gaumont, changed over to bingo. Although closed for some years awaiting deliberations over its future by the local borough, who own the whole 'Aggie' complex, the building retains much of its original plasterwork and is of the greatest interest.

The London Pavilion has been
a cinema since 1934

*Left* The Kilburn Empire of
1899 enjoying life as the
Essoldo cinema in 1969

*Right* Two years later the front
had been re-faced and the
original auditorium smashed
to bits to form a Classic cinema

The remaining London theatres in this selection are all later cinema conversions of larger and more ornate theatre buildings. The London Pavilion on Piccadilly Circus has been a cinema since 1934. First built in 1885 by Saunders and Worley, the interior was reconstructed in 1900 by Wylson and Long, and then again in 1934 for the cinema use by Frank Matcham's office. The present interior (soon due for reconstruction and subdivision) retains its theatrical form with an upper circle, but is entirely plain.

The Kilburn Empire is regrettably an object lesson in how best to maltreat an old theatre. Built in 1899 to the designs of Palgrave and Company and Wylson and Long, this theatre was designed to be both music hall and circus, with a seating capacity of nearly 2000. It became a full-time cinema in 1928, being later renamed the Essoldo, and survived substantially unchanged inside and out until 1971, when it was sold and its interest effectively destroyed in a series of alteration works from which it emerged as the Classic cinema in 1972. The exterior was completely clad in metal sheet (a familiar 'Classic' trademark), and a new small cinema created as a self-contained 'cell' within the consequentially mutilated theatre auditorium. All that escaped unscathed was the stage area with its extremely rare elephant pits below and animal traps in the stage itself. The transformation of the old Kilburn Empire was an act of singularly wanton destruction.

A handful of other suburban London examples remain to be described. The Elephant and Castle Theatre first opened in 1872, but was reconstructed in 1879 to the designs of J. T. Robinson, and completed after his death by his son-in-law Frank Matcham, his first theatre building at the age of 27. It became a cinema in 1928; complete reconstruction followed in 1931 and today it is the ABC, Elephant and Castle, distinguished neither as a theatre or cinema. Yet another Matcham theatre is the Borough in Stratford East. Built in 1895, this was reconstructed in 1930 and given a new corner cinema front as well as a streamlined interior more appropriate to films. It is an oddly effective mixture, the bulk of the old brick theatre, with the name Borough still visible above the shopping frontage, contrasted with the white, typically thirties, cinema entrance. Inside it is now more the Rex cinema than the Borough theatre (or, to be strictly accurate, the Rex bingo), but not without interest. The bingo hall closed in 1979 and at the time of writing the whole building was under threat of redevelopment.

The Grand Theatre on St John's Hill, Clapham Junction was opened on 19 November 1900 by Dan Leno. It was designed by E. A. Woodrow, architect of the famous Collins Music Hall in Islington. It was a Palace of Varieties rich in theatrical lore, and seated 3000, but it became a full-time cinema in 1927, later Essoldo, and remained one until bingo took over in the late sixties. The outside is no masterpiece, but is certainly an outstandingly massive example of vulgar redbrick and terracotta splendour in the baroque style, and it prepares one more than adequately for what sets the Grand apart from most other theatres, its Chinese-style interior. In spite of a false ceiling above the dress circle level, much of the plaster decoration survives, including the pagoda boxes guarded by dragons, and above the false ceiling, the original ceiling dome in the form of 'an inverted willow pattern plate'. The present bingo club is a poor apology for what was once perhaps the most important of London's suburban Edwardian music halls, and demolition and redevelopment are threatened in the near future.

The use of theatres as cinemas was, if anything, even more general in Scotland than in England. The earliest indoor demonstration of moving pictures in Scotland was at the Empire Palace Theatre. Edinburgh on Monday 13 April 1896, and two of the earliest recorded theatre conversions to cinema use were also in Edinburgh. These were at the Palladium Theatre in East Fountainbridge, originally built as Cooke's Circus in 1886, which became a cinema in 1912 (now completely altered), and the Princess's Theatre in Nicholson Street of 1862 by D. McGibbon, which became the La Scala Electric Theatre in 1912. This has also been very much altered. Still in Edinburgh, the Grand Theatre in St Stephen's Street, Stockbridge of 1901 by T. P. Marwick was the Grand Picture House from 1920 until 1960 (it is now a Tiffany's Dance Hall); and the Alhambra Theatre of Varieties in Leith Walk and the Capitol Theatre in Manderston

A mid-twenties conversion to cinema use by John Alexander of an old theatre in Gateshead. The Moorish details overlaid the typical Edwardian fibrous plasterwork

Street, Leith were both designed in 1914 by J. M. Johnston for the dual purpose of theatre and cinema. The first has been closed now for 20 years, and the other is a bingo hall.

In Glasgow, the recently demolished (in spite of being listed) Palace Theatre in Gorbals Street had an extraordinary Indian-style interior of 1905 and had been a cinema for nearly half a century. The Coliseum in Laurieston, Gorbals, still a cinema, is in essence a theatre of 1904 by Frank Matcham, but the façade has been altered and the interior gutted. The Olympia in Bridgeton, now the ABC cinema, with its fine sandstone façade, was designed in 1910 by J. M. Arthur. In Dundee, half of the old Gaiety Theatre in Victoria Road, extended in 1903 by William Alexander, is now the Victoria cinema. The King's Theatre and Hippodrome in Cowgate, designed in 1909–12 by Frank Thomson, has been gutted and converted into the Gaumont cinema.

It is in Dumfries where the earliest documented change from theatre to cinema occurred. This was at the Theatre Royal in 1909. This theatre is in many ways historically the most interesting in Scotland, as it is the only Georgian survival in the country, dating originally from 1790–2 and designed by Thomas Boyd, and altered in 1876 by C. J. Phipps. Cinema use continued from 1909 until 1954, and after restoration the building has reverted to theatrical use. In Falkirk the Grand Theatre of 1903 by A.

45

Cullen was converted into a cinema in 1934 in which use the heavily altered building remains. The Alexandra Theatre in Greenock of 1905 by the same architect later became an Odeon cinema, but was demolished in 1973. And in Motherwell, the New Century Theatre of 1902, again by A. Cullen, became the Rex cinema in the thirties and was given a new frontage. Four other theatres which are still cinemas are the King's Theatre, Kilmarnock (1904); the King's Theatre, Kirkcaldy (1905–6 by Swanston and Syme); the Opera House, Lochgelly (1900); and the Dunbeath Theatre of Varieties in Methil (1908 by Swanston and Syme).

It is not hard to find the reason why so many theatres became cinemas at an early date. As films became better and their attendant variety turns more elaborate, so public demand for venues to see the film shows far outstripped the supply. In the early days purpose-built cinemas were still not all that numerous, and hired or converted public halls were the most popular solution with the showmen. But it was nothing like as satisfactory an arrangement as using the existing theatres, with their ready-made 'fantasy' atmospheres and sense of occasion, and also their instant availability of stages, dressing room accommodation for variety acts and comfortable seating for the patrons. It was an obvious progression by entrepreneurs and promoters to utilise the legitimate theatre and music halls, and to convert them into full-time picture houses. It was the same

The Balham Empire (1900) was the earliest full-time conversion to cinema use in London. Demolished 1974

46

A photograph of the early 1920s showing the Surrey Theatre in Blackfriars Road, London in cinema use. Demolished 1934

type of reasoning in the twenties and early thirties that led to the second wave of theatre conversions, when again it was the public clamour for ever bigger and better picture palaces that resulted in many of the larger and more elaborate theatres being turned over to permanent cinema use in order to realise their most profitable potential.

47

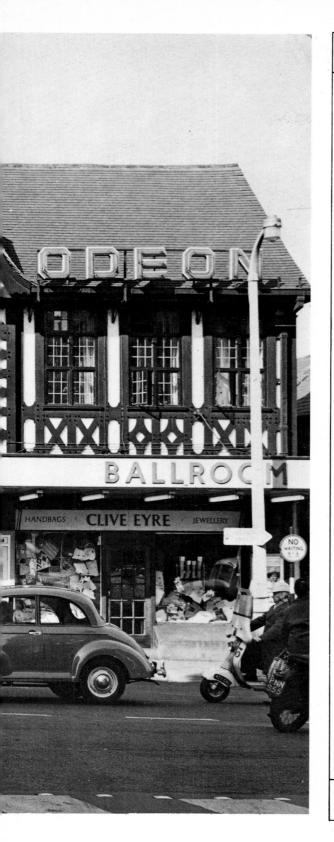

# 3

# THE 'SILENT' TWENTIES

The picture theatre supplies folk with the flavour of romance for which they crave.

THEODORE KOMISARJEVSKY, 1931

T HE FIRST WORLD WAR meant a virtual cessation of cinema building, and in the years immediately following 1918 little was commenced because of the restrictions on construction. Thus it cannot really be said that the cinema developed at all in Britain between 1914 and 1921. However a demand for new cinemas was building up, since in the absence of any marked activity in British film studios, the American corporations were saturating the British market. Most of all the Americans introduced in this period the process known as 'block booking', where the same film can be shown throughout the same area in any number of cinemas. It opened up new vistas of the market in 1921 and created a new demand; today the system remains with us as one of the best reasons for the declining cinema.

In 1921 the *Kine Year Book* estimated that there were about 4000 of the early cinemas in existence in Britain, mostly plain rectangular open halls with a small seating capacity of 300–600 on one level only; and it was estimated that another 2000 cinemas were needed to satisfy the public demand. With the lifting of building restrictions coupled to this new

*On previous page* The freakish half-timbered elevation of the Picture House (now Odeon) in Chesterfield, opened in 1923. It was designed to blend in with the famous parish church

Suburban cinema architecture as it was by 1918: the Ritz, Surbiton, Surrey

A more dour northern
equivalent of the example in
Surbiton: the Abbeydale
cinema, Sheffield (1922).

demand, cinemas generally became much larger, being provided with circles and overall usually designed in the traditions of late Victorian and Edwardian theatres. It was also in 1921 that the first cinema of outstanding architectural importance by a major architect was built in England: it was the Regent in Brighton, designed by Robert Atkinson, recently demolished. If one does not accept that the 'super' cinema only came in with the talkies in 1928, then the Regent has a fair claim to be considered the first British super cinema to be built.

Robert Atkinson was a most distinguished architect and teacher, who considered the cinema as a building to be a great aesthetic and architectural challenge to the abilities of the architect. As P. Morton Shand puts it in his highly subjective 1930 book *Modern Theatres and Cinemas*, 'the first- or anyhow the first notable-English cinema to be designed by "a qualified architect" was Mr. Robert Atkinson's "Regent" (an appropriate name at last!) in Brighton. It had considerable decorative charm . . .'. Atkinson was a very skilled designer who had worked on theatres and cinemas before 1914 in partnership with George Alexander, and after his partner's death in the war, the practice continued in Atkinson's name. The Regent was thus the first of a long line of fine cinemas in the twenties that paved the way for the talkies and the super cinemas of the thirties. It was a classic design in traditional mould with much decorative plasterwork and indeed too many fake columns which impeded sightlines, but it was the result of Atkinson's first-hand study of early theatres and cinemas by architects such as Thomas Lamb in America. In fact after a fire in 1928, the Regent was restored in even more grandiose fashion, but its long decline in the 1960s and 1970s was both tragic and unnecessary.

Europe's largest cinema of this period sprang up in the unlikely setting of the London suburb of Acton. Called the Globe, it was designed by G. Perry Pratt, and cost about £125,000 to build. Seating capacity was 2500 and the rich interior, an uneasy compromise between Greek and Roman styles, had a large organ and full orchestral facilities. The Globe opened on 26 March 1921 and closed for demolition in the early 1960's.

Typical of developments in the provinces is Portsmouth, where seven cinemas were built between 1921 and 1924 to add to an already impressive array of pre-1914 halls. The Majestic Picture House, later the Essoldo, at Kingston Cross still survives and is a splendid building which cost £50,000 to erect. Although its licence was granted on 14 February 1922 for a seating capacity of 1286 to a Mr R. Stokes, no drawings have survived to indicate the designer of a stuccoed classical façade that boldly places a segmental pediment directly beneath a triangular pediment, and a galleried interior carried on Doric columns that is as ornate in its plasterwork as any Edwardian music hall. After continuous use until 6 December 1973, the cinema came under threat from conversion into a snooker club. In an unsuccessful bid to persuade the Government to list the building, the Portsmouth City Architect went so far as to describe the building as 'a by-product of the Hollywood "dream factory" and Portsmouth's only real surviving cinema of that tremendously vigorous and romantic period'. Such brave words were of no avail and in due course the circle was mutilated in the conversion works, although the greater part of the cinema's plasterwork still survives.

The astonishing Moorish exterior of the Palace in Portsmouth. 1921 by A. E. Cogswell

By far the most interesting cinema built in Portsmouth in this period was the Palace, in Commercial Road, right in the centre of the city, opposite the Theatre Royal and adjacent to the Guildhall. It opened on 21 February 1921 and the *Portsmouth Evening News* commented that it made 'a splendid addition to the long list of amusement houses in Portsmouth . . . it is adequately equipped with all the modern apparatus of an up-to-date picture house, and with its carpeted floors and velvet corded seats provides the last word in comfort for patrons . . . there was a general expression of delight on all lips'. Several things distinguish the Palace as being out of the run of usual early twenties cinemas. First its architect is known, and the original drawings survive: he was A. E. Cogswell, a prominent local architect, chiefly known for his magnificent Portsmouth public houses for Messrs Brickwoods. Moreover, he is known to have designed eight local cinemas, of which the Palace is the last survivor. From the planning aspect, it is also unusual in that it is back to front with the entrances from the foyer to the auditorium sited each side and under the screen. Externally it is most curious of all, being frankly Indian in style with five domes and minarets, and Moorish arched windows as an added bonus. Hardly a triumph of architectural merit, it is surely unique for its date, and fully in line with the long British tradition of seaside piers and buildings for entertainment. Having emerged victorious from a Public Inquiry in 1975 into its Compulsory Purchase for demolition by the City Council, it is still remarkably unaltered, complete down to its external paybox. However, unprotected as a listed building, its future remains ever precarious.

Leslie Kemp, one of the most respected of senior architects who worked on cinema designs, recalls that after qualifying from the Architectural Association in London in 1922 he was able to obtain employment with Andrew Mather, who designed the original Capitol cinema in Haymarket, London (altered by W. E. Trent in 1928 into the Gaumont, and later demolished and replaced in 1962 by the present basement Odeon). Incidentally Andrew Mather, later to achieve much fame with his Odeon designs, was like so many of his contemporaries such as Frank Matcham, W. G. R. Sprague, W. E. Trent and E. A. Stone not in fact a qualified architect at all. For his design work with Mather (which included typing and general office work), Leslie Kemp was paid the princely sum of £2.00 per week, and in 1924 he went to work for W. E. Trent 'being desirous of obtaining remuneration more commensurate with my labours'. Here he worked on the new Gaumonts being erected in Brighton, Bournemouth, Preston, Sheffield and Bristol, all lavish picture palaces complete with full stage facilities.

Each city was acquiring at least one really elaborate cinema right in its heart. Manchester had the Piccadilly, designed by Percy Hothersall in 1922; Hull had the Carlton, designed by Blackmore and Sykes; and Nottingham had the Elite, dating from 1921 and costing £100,000 to build, an especially ostentatious white faience-faced classical block of buildings containing a superb auditorium, a ballroom, restaurant, shops and offices.

However, it was not perhaps until 1923 that the cinema achieved any substantive accolade of respectability as a work of architecture. Frank T. Verity, FRIBA won the RIBA bronze medal for the best frontage in London completed during the year 1923 with his design for the Shepherd's Bush Pavilion. The jury was nothing if not distinguished, including such luminaries as Sir Edwin Lutyens and Guy Dawber and they found the Pavilion an 'imposing structure of brick and stone in which the former material expecially is used with great imagination'. Frank Verity is a key figure in the development of early 20th-century cinema and theatre design. He was born in 1864 and educated at Cranleigh and privately in Richmond and Boulogne. His architectural and art training was cosmopolitan and a fitting preparation for what was to come later, being successively at the Royal College of Art, University College, the Architectural Association and the Royal Academy in London, with a

One of the first of the new
style picture palaces: the
Carlton, Hull, designed by
Blackmore and Sykes in the
mid-twenties. Note the
inscription above the
proscenium: 'A picture is a
poem without words'

The cinema achieves
respectability. The Pavilion,
Shepherd's Bush (now the
Odeon) won the 1923 RIBA
medal for the best frontage in
London for its architect, Frank
T. Verity

period of study in Paris. He travelled extensively during this time in Italy, France, Germany, America and Canada; and was a pupil of R. Phené-Spiers before being articled to his father. This could hardly have been a better introduction to theatre and cinema design, for his father was one of the most respected of Victorian theatre architects in London, designing, for example, the Criterion Theatre in 1874 and the Comedy Theatre in 1881, still two of the best preserved Victorian playhouses in Britain. In partnership with his father, Frank designed several important public buildings in London, and after his father's death went into practice himself about 1900, and succeeded his father as architect to the Lord Chamberlain's Department. During the Edwardian era he designed a number of important theatres, notably the Scala, Imperial and old Empire theatres in London, the Theatre Royal, Bath and the Theatre Royal, Windsor. It was a natural progression to the world of cinema design, and his first cinema was the original New Gallery Kinema in London's Regent Street in 1912, afterwards rebuilt by Nicholas and Dixon-Spain in 1923–5. He next designed the Electric Pavilion, Marble Arch in 1914, but it was the Shepherd's Bush Pavilion in 1923 that made his reputation in the field. It was a splendid, if conservative, exercise in Verity's favoured Italianate Renaissance style, designed for the cinema entrepreneur Israel Davis, and won warm praise at the time from all quarters. It had in fact been designed several years previously, during the war, so it can be fairly counted as the earliest of the really large sumptuous cinemas to leave the drawing board. The main thing it proved in London was a 3000 seat auditorium in a rather run-down suburb could successfully play regularly to packed houses. The Pavilion was badly damaged by bombing in the last war and was not restored until 1954–5 with a completely simplified interior by Samuel Beverley, G. E. Skeats and Sir Anthony Denny. The still immensely impressive brick and stone classical exterior, with its

Plan of the Shepherd's Bush Pavilion

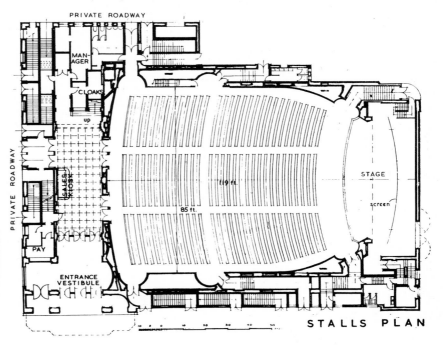

STALLS PLAN

55

Frank Verity at his Italian Renaissance best. The Plaza, Lower Regent Street, London (1926) showing the corner now obliterated by advertising. The interior also has been destroyed by 'twinning'

Original drawing by Frank Verity showing the front of the Carlton in London's Haymarket. Designed as a theatre, it became a cinema within three years of its opening in 1927

barrel-vaulted roof and austere cliffs of beautifully crafted brickwork, was virtually unharmed and unaltered in the reconstruction. Renamed the Gaumont upon reopening in 1955, the seating was reduced to 2036, but since then the Pavilion has changed name again to Odeon, and been further altered and subdivided for bingo and a much smaller cinema.

The Samuel Beverley of the 1954 reconstruction was Verity's son-in-law and they had gone into partnership in 1930. Prior to this Beverley assisted Verity in several important London cinemas, including the Astoria, Charing Cross Road (1927) and the Plaza in Lower Regent Street (1926), a superb classical Italian interior in the best Thomas Lamb tradition that on any account deserved to survive intact, but was ruthlessly cut into two in 1968. There was also the beautiful, and in many ways unique, Carlton Theatre in Haymarket, designed in 1926 and opened early in 1927. The superbly proportioned and simple Italianate interior of this theatre (in fact a cinema for all but three years of its life) was only destroyed in 1978 after a long, hard fought but ultimately unsuccessful preservation battle.

Frank Verity can be said without doubt to have been the first British cinema architect of any international importance. He designed the new Vaudeville Theatre in Paris, and upon becoming the chief architect for the Paramount Picture Corporation, designed the Paramount cinema there. In Britain he designed the key Paramount cinemas in London's Tottenham Court Road, Birmingham, Leeds, Liverpool, Manchester, Newcastle and Glasgow, a group of buildings that have all suffered grievously in the battle for survival through a world war and subsequent ravages of developers and 'improvers'. In partnership with Samuel Beverley in the 1930s he designed the Palace Theatre, Bristol; the Gaumont, Peckham; the Regal, Southampton; and the Ritz cinemas in Aldershot, Bexhill, Nottingham and Richmond, to name but a few of the most prominent. The Ritz, Richmond was his last design before he died on 14 August 1937, and he was not alive to see it open. He would have been heartened to see its beautiful classical brick front façade, but mortified to see it close on 11 December 1971, prior to demolition to make way for an office development.

Frank Verity was an architect of the highest ability in all fields of design, not least for his blocks of luxury flats in London which revolutionised their planning early this century. Goodhart-Rendel wrote an appreciation of Verity in the *RIBA Journal* on 16 October 1937 which sums up his achievements in the fields of theatre and cinema with all this justly famous architectural writer's command of the language:

French reasonableness marks everything that Mr. Verity did, although the style of his most frequent choice was not French, but Italian. In the year 1889 he won the Tite Prize for his design for a theatre in the Venetian style of the sixteenth century, and never did a student win that prize with a design more prophetic of what he was afterwards to execute in practice. The interiors of the Imperial (now pulled down) and of his Scala Theatre, link this prize design naturally with his comparatively recent cinemas, the Plaza and the Carlton. All are Italian and all are architecturally most successful . . . Mr. Verity's more sumptuous cinemas are examples of such high architectural accomplishment that anyone is to be pitied who cannot enjoy them for their own sake. In designing them he did what he never failed to do, he dignified the requirements of his employers by the art he expended in supplying them.

Throughout the twenties, it has to be said that until Wamsley Lewis's New Victoria cinema opened in 1930, British architects seemed almost totally unaware of the work of the great theatre and cinema designers such as Hans Poelzig, Fritz Wilms or Mendelsohn in Germany, or the almost equally significant 'modern' designs being produced in Scandinavia. The first glimmerings of appreciation of Continental work are to be found in the designs of Julian R. Leathart and W. F. Granger. In the words of P. Morton Shand, Leathart was 'our foremost cinema architect', but only because he was in Shand's opinion evidently the best of a very bad bunch! Leathart and Granger's first cinema design to catch the eye of critical, as well as public, approval was the Kensington cinema in London's High Street, Kensington, which opened in 1926. To quote Shand again, writing in 1930, 'So uninspired, indeed, are our "Picture Palaces" – the very name seems to foredoom designers to false values – that the "Kensington Cinema", in spite of being a shocking breach of architectural manners, having regard to its site, till lately ranked among them as one of

The Kensington cinema (now Odeon) in High Street, Kensington, by Leathart and Granger 1926. One of the few twenties cinemas besides the Shepherd's Bush Pavilion to win critical approval

the more interesting and encouraging designs'. When opened, it seated 2300 and was claimed to be the largest cinema in England. Today, renamed the Odeon, and with its interior mutilated and subdivided, it seems a very modest, unadventurous cinema indeed. However, the exterior is little changed and its austere, plain, neo-classical façade is undeniably well proportioned in its slightly Germanic coolness. There has been a recurrent threat of redevelopment hanging over the building for the last decade.

It was the group of three cinemas designed by Leathart and Granger in Richmond, Sheen and Twickenham at the end of the twenties that mark them as being quite above the average run of cinema designers. The Richmond cinema (now the Odeon) is an early 'atmospheric' (see beginning of chapter 4); it is also the only one to remain intact today. The finest of the trio, the Sheen cinema, was demolished in the early sixties to make way for an office-block. Although the Sheen cinema (which opened in 1930) had a relatively conventional interior, the exterior was a *tour de force* of art deco motifs mainly in artificial stone, used in a manner quite unlike any other cinema design, but finding some parallel in the treatment, both inside and out, of the Savoy Theatre in London's Strand, completed the previous year to the designs of Frank A. Tugwell and Basil Ionides. The other cinema of the trio, the Twickenham was designed in 1929, and disappeared long ago, yet another victim of speculative commercial redevelopment. It had a notably cool and modernistic exterior that P. Morton Shand considered 'by far the best façade which any English cinema yet built can boast, and one of the few that can sustain comparison with current Continental examples'.

A number of architectural practices made their name in the early and mid-twenties, designing the new, larger picture palaces. In the northwest, George E. Tonge was especially prolific, and Horace G. Bradley designed a number of prominent examples in Birmingham. James Forbes designed the Capitol, Middlesborough; E. H. Walker the Picture House in Doncaster; and Bullock and Jeeves were responsible for the Victory cinema, Loughborough; all in 1920. Another prolific practice in the north was Schofield and Berry, and in Liverpool George L. Alexander joined forces with Messrs Watson, Landless and Pearce to design the Prince of Wales cinema in 1920. The same year Stocks, Sykes and Hickson designed the Grand Picture Theatre in Huddersfield. Two fine cinemas also made their appearance in Cardiff, the New Cinema in Bute Street, designed by Percy Thomas and Ivor Jones, and the Penylon by Wilmott and Smith.

Several other cinemas deserve brief notice in the period immediately preceding the advent of the talkies. Green's Playhouse in Glasgow, now called the Apollo, opened in 1925 with 4400 seats, at that time the largest capacity of any cinema outside America. The interior, much altered over the years, was designed by John Fairweather and decorated by John Alexander, of whom more in chapter 5.

A remarkably early example of conservation planning occurred in Chesterfield, Derbyshire where it was insisted that the new Picture House in Holywell Street, opposite the celebrated Parish Church with its crooked spire, should blend in with its historic surroundings. The result is an unique gabled half-timbered façade that looks as if it has wandered over the border from Cheshire or Herefordshire. The Picture House, which opened on 10 September 1923, later to be taken over in 1936 and become an Odeon, remains virtually untouched. Although only seating 900, it had a large restaurant and ballroom (now a disco-club), and full stage facilities, and even the fly-tower was half-timbered externally!

In 1927 the Davis family, who had built the Shepherd's Bush Pavilion, decided to build an even larger palace in the suburbs of south London, and to name it after their cinema circuit. The result was the Davis' Theatre, Croydon, and its designer was Robert Cromie, not by any means the most imaginative of cinema architects, but the one destined to become about the most prolific of designers for independent circuits in the thirties. It opened in December 1928, just at the time that the first talkies were being introduced to England. It was vast and it was ornate, the interior being described as 'modern French decorative work' and it was designed to seat nearly 4000, making it the largest auditorium in England. The usual extravagant claims were made for it at its opening, including the description that it was the most ambitious project of its kind in Europe. That it may have been in cost, but in design it was certainly sub-Verity, and in any case paid no regard whatever to European 'modern' cinema design. It was of course intended to ape the supers of Thomas

Lamb in America, which it did to good effect with its great marble entrance foyer and galleried rotunda, its domed auditorium and its Portland stone and gilded metal exterior. However, by 1928 this was all becoming distinctly old-fashioned, and the New Victoria cinema was already on the horizon. Today the Davis' has gone, replaced by the usual panoply of sixties High Street commercialism.

Also opened at the end of 1928 in London was the first of A. E. Abrahams's celebrated Regal circuit. This was the Regal, Marble Arch, designed by Clifford A. Aish, with an interior of amazing elaboration with painted murals and gilded plasterwork in the manner of Thomas Lamb, and garlands of foliage, a pergola and lighting effects in the best John Eberson atmospheric manner. The intended effect was that of a Roman amphitheatre, and in truth it was a piece of monumental vulgarity without any overriding style or sense of aesthetic taste. This has also been destroyed and replaced by one of London's least satisfactory office developments, occupying a key place in the townscape at the head of Park Lane, with a plain apology for a cinema underneath it.

It was really the case that throughout the twenties architects sought unsuccessfully for a recognisable style for the cinema. The buildings became bigger and bigger, and ever more elaborate, but they failed to register any intrinsic character that was immediately divorced from the theatre tradition, and all too often they were simply a lumpish and rather unstylish intrusion into the townscape of almost every urban scene in Britain. It was at this time, just as the talkies arrived, that an editorial in *The Architects' Journal* lamented that

The conclusion to which I am driven is that our exhibitors as a body have not yet awakened to the commercial importance of architecture. There are cinemas in which a quantitative excess of architecture tries to make up for a qualitative poverty that is often pitiable. There are others (and these are far more numerous) in which to witness a film is like eating out of a newspaper.

P. Morton Shand was just as scathing in 1930:

The newer ad hoc buildings more often vie with one another in that nouveau riche ostentation which their patrons are invited to envisage as the 'last word in luxury'. . . . The design of our cinemas is part of the heavy price we pay for our public neglect of architecture . . . The desire of the film exhibitor being usually to disguise his picture theatre as a showman's booth, it is not surprising that British architects have so far had no adequate chance of trying to discover the cinema's most logical and satisfactory structural form.

Referring to American cinema design, he commented, 'In America, which, perhaps naturally, has remained our standard model in these respects, the meaningless parade of garish glitter has likewise been carried as far as the almighty dollar can carry it'. Thomas Lamb's solitary British commission to rebuild the Empire Theatre in Leicester Square, London, in partnership with Frank Matcham, was labelled 'the monstrous fruit of an Anglo-American collaboration', a 'glorified gin-palace', and 'one of the most supremely parvenu buildings in the world'. The hapless Marble Arch Regal, described above, is damned as 'strident bedizenment'. Shand goes on 'this building's complacently swaggering display of "the modern style" can be compared to the parodies of Savile Row sobriety which are exhibited in the shop windows of Strand tailoring establishments labelled "latest West-End cut". The Regal looks as if it had been dressed for its part as a flash gigolo by some "Alexander the Great" of the Edgware Road'.

For all Shand's arrogant self-gratification as a man who knows a well-turned phrase when he writes it, there is a kernel of truth in his pronouncements. The great decade of the American cinema designs had all but passed before the golden age began in Britain with the advent of the talkies, and at the same time the Continental scene in Europe was steadfastly ignored in the twenties.

In Germany the outstanding cinema specialist was Fritz Wilms of the celebrated UFA Company, who designed a number of cinemas in a splendidly unfussy and direct manner in the years following 1924 and

'Night Architecture'. The Titania-Palast in Berlin by Schöffler, Schlönbach and Jacobi (late twenties)

The atmospheric simplicity of a large German cinema of the twenties: the Mercedes-Palast in Berlin by Fritz Wilms

which also, significantly, cost a great deal less per cubic foot than their American or British counterparts. Fritz Wilms's Piccadilly Theatre in Berlin was an excellent example of the Kinos or Lichtspielhäuser where 'night architecture' was a factor of major importance. 'Night architecture' simply expressed the idea that films were a night-time entertainment by means of illuminated lettering and extensive areas of glass in the façade that showed up areas of the internal activity after dark. It was a sufficiently Germanic idea to be only fully exploited in Britain at the Odeon in London's Leicester Square, although, to be fair, the whole idea of the illuminated Odeon advertising towers was a step towards 'night architecture'. Wilms was an architect whose work owed much to Oscar Kaufmann and his pioneering Cines in Berlin of 1911, but like his contemporaries he used concrete extensively and boldly in his interiors. Simplicity was the order of the day, with none of the applied frills and decorations that characterised American and British movie palaces. Fritz Wilms's most celebrated cinema designs were the UFA cinema in Turmstrasse, Berlin; the Luna Filmpalast, Berlin; the Mercedes-Palast, also in Berlin; and the UFA-Schauburg in Magdeburg.

The German architects who designed cinemas were mostly well established or even celebrated in other fields, none more so than Erich Mendelsohn. His Universum or Luxor-Palast was built in Berlin in 1926–9. Curiously, its highly successful great horseshoe shaped auditorium with balcony was to be decisive in influencing Continental cinema planning in the opposite direction towards the open stadium type, almost invariably without a separate circle. Hans Poelzig was the most spectacular of the German designers and his Grosses Schauspielhaus of 1919 in Berlin was to be of great influence on the young Wamsley Lewis when he spent some time in Germany in 1927–8 before designing the New Victoria Theatre in London. Poelzig also designed the Babylon cinema in Berlin in 1928, a masterly example of the early use of re-inforced concrete in an absolutely plain auditorium seating 1200.

Friedrich Lipp was the German architect who occasionally came nearest to introducing the kind of elaborate decoration being used in other countries. His finest cinema was the Capitol at Breslau, a perfect example of 'night architecture' as well as boasting a monumental auditorium with much use of art deco shapes in the roof form. He also designed the Atrium in Berlin, where the auditorium ceiling was extremely elaborately lit.

The German cinema designs in their totally up-to-date modernity and simplicity, with no concessions to traditional decoration, really only find any parallel in Scandinavia. In Britain their inspiration surfaced just twice, first in the New Victoria, and secondly, some years later in 1934 in the heart of London's Mayfair in the Curzon designed by Sir John Burnet, Tait and Lorne.

Things were more traditional in France, and it is only in Paris that any cinema is sufficiently out of the ordinary to merit special attention. Apart from the efforts of Frank Verity for Paramount, the Gaumont Corporation employed Henri Belloc in 1930 to reconstruct the existing Gaumont Palace into a 6000 seat answer to the American Roxy. Earlier in the twenties, commendable restraint had been displayed by Raymond Fischer in his Cluny cinema, and by Henri Sauvage in the Gambetta cinema where the screen was surrounded by murals of almost art nouveau exoticism. The modernistic restraint was continued in 1931 by the Gaumont Company in their showpiece cinema on the Champs-Elysées called the Alhambra, designed by Georges Gumpel, Gray and Evans, but generally Parisian cinemas followed American precedents. The atmospherics did not come to Paris until 1932 when John Eberson designed the 4000 seat Moroccan style Rex cinema, still almost intact, in collaboration with a local architect, and examples soon followed in the principal provincial cities.

Elsewhere in Europe cinema designs were no more distinctive, although Amsterdam was able to boast of a superb and prophetic art deco cinema in the form of the Tuschinski, which was opened in 1918. Abraham Tuschinski was a Polish Jew who had opened his first cinema in Rotterdam in 1909, and he employed Hyman Louis de Jong as his architect to design his art deco fantasy. The results were certainly fantastic and to this day references to the 'Tuschinski' style are used as a term of architectural abuse in Holland. The entrance façade is church-like, and romantically art deco with flanking towers, all faced in faience tiling. Internally the foyer, decorated by Jaap Gidding, is the best feature, as the auditorium has been much altered by successive modernisation works. Overall, the Tuschinski is a fascinating, if somewhat overrated building.

Scandinavia, however, had more to offer. In Stockholm in 1922 Gunnar Asplund designed the Skandia cinema, a classic and uniquely beautiful example of the successful compromise between early modern design and the more romantic elements of the theatre. It was, as P. Morton Shand admiringly commented, 'an example of that elegant modernism which we envy the Scandinavians for having evolved so naturally and, as it seems, effortlessly, from the lifeless classicism of the nineteenth century'. Nothing remotely comparable occurred in any British cinema. In spite of its old-fashioned rectangular shape and resultant poor sightlines, the Skandia was architecturally unquestionably a triumph, and the inspiration for another key Scandinavian cinema, the Alexandra in Copenhagen by V. H. Hammar. This was simpler and more modern, with a sparingly effective use of figures and motifs reminiscent of the best of art deco.

Throughout the old British Empire, cinema design followed the more traditional course inspired by America. South Africa had a particularly fine example in the tudor-style Playhouse Theatre, which became a cinema, in Smith Street, Durban, and there is the equally superb atmospheric Alhambra in Cape Town, opened in 1931. New Zealand had the Civic cinema in Auckland, an astonishing atmospheric Hindu Temple of 1929 by Bohringer, Taylor and Johnson. Australia spawned many spectacular cinemas. A good number of them were even more the epitome of bad taste than their American predecessors, and they are all faithfully charted by Ross Thorne in his excellent *Picture Palace Architecture in Australia* (1976). Suffice it to say here that no cinema in Australia exceeded Sir John Betjeman's beloved State in Sydney, a veritable 'Cathedral of the Motion Picture', designed in 1929 by Henry White after sketches by John Eberson. It was not in fact a true atmospheric. The main foyer in the English Gothic baronial style has more than a hint of Komisarjevsky's foyer at the Granada in the London suburb of Tooting that followed it a year later. Elsewhere the styles varied with alarming facility from Louis to

South Africa's finest
atmospheric: the Alhambra,
Cape Town. (1931, architect
Roger Cooke)

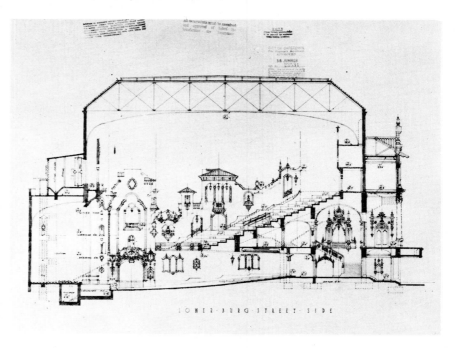

Architect's sectional drawing
of the Alhambra, Cape Town

The atmospheric Hindu extravaganza of the Civic cinema, Auckland, New Zealand. (1929 by Bohringer, Taylor and Johnson)

Auditorium of State cinema, Sydney, Australia. Designed by Henry White 'after sketches by John Eberson'

Louis, but above all the State, Sydney became the symbol of the Australian super cinema. Nothing else approached it for magnificence, but attention must briefly be also drawn to Henry White's other collaboration with John Eberson at the Capitol, Sydney in 1928, a cinema called at the time the 'House of Dreams'. There was also the State, Melbourne of 1929, designed by Bohringer, Taylor and Johnson, an amazing Moorish atmospheric both inside and out. Seating 3300, it was the largest cinema ever built in Australia. Finally mention must also be made of Hoyt's famous Regent circuit, principally those in Sydney, Adelaide, Melbourne and South Yarra, all designed by Ballantyne and Hare.

And so the scene is now set for an examination of the source of these extravagances, the American dream palaces and how they came to Britain.

# 'AN ACRE OF SEATS IN A GARDEN OF DREAMS'

It is here that the royal nabobs and lords gather to barter and exchange everything from fruit to human souls.

JOHN EBERSON describing the Avalon cinema, Chicago in 1927

As with so many aspects of British and Western European life and society, good and bad, it was the American model that provided the later inspiration on this side of the Atlantic. The great American movie palaces of the 1920s were copied with diligence in the succeeding decade, nowhere more so than in England. As these vast American buildings took shape, and they were never to be equalled or exceeded in size, so two schools of thought developed about their design. These twenties cinema designs, broadly speaking, fell into two groups, one typifying the use of neo-classical forms and detail (known euphemistically as the 'hard-top' school), and the other being altogether more imaginative by experimenting with complex lighting effects in an entirely artificial setting. Thus the feeling of being in the open air was frequently the objective; the experience of the hanging Italian gardens, or perhaps the excitement of being surrounded by a Moorish town. These were the atmospherics. Each of these schools of thought had its hero: Thomas W. Lamb, a Scottish-born architect, was the unquestioned leader of the neo-classical architects, and John Eberson, an Austrian who trained in Europe and later emigrated to America, represented the atmospheric school.

The scene for this classic conflict of architectural and design ideologies had been set in the decade 1910–20, when the movie craze in America had really taken off. Known not altogether affectionately as 'movie madness', it has been estimated that by 1915 over 25,000 picture theatres had been opened in America with an average daily audience of six million people! The cinema may have had a short history in terms of years, but its effects on society have at times been almost cataclysmic.

As in Britain, very many of the old theatre buildings in the larger towns were converted into cinema use, with films forming an important part of that uniquely American phenomenon, the vaudeville shows. But more and more buildings were being erected exclusively for cinema use, and these were known as 'Pictureplay Theatres', being also usually situated in the suburbs rather than the centres of towns and cities. In the centres most new cinema buildings continued to have full stage facilities provided, for the vaudeville tradition died hard in America. It should also be remembered that in America, movie palaces were almost always known as 'theatres', leaving no distinction in their title between them and the live theatres.

The first American building devoted exclusively to showing films was in Pittsburgh (1905), but more typical of the early years is the Bijou Theatre in Knoxville, Tennessee, which opened on 8 March 1909. Designed by an architect named Oakley from Montgomery, Alabama, it was intended to be exclusively a live theatre. However, as early as 1912 screen and projection equipment were installed.

Another example is the Majestic Theatre in Dubuque, Iowa which opened in 1910, and after long neglect, was magnificently restored and re-opened in March 1976 as the Five Flags Theatre. Although only a small 750 seat auditorium, it is remarkable as being the earliest surviving work of the great theatre-designing partnership of C. W. and George L. Rapp, whose names will occur again. Like the Bijou, the Majestic also went over to cinema use, when in 1933 it became the Orpheum.

The career of Thomas W. Lamb began in 1909 with the City Theatre

68

on 14th Street in New York, designed for William Fox, but it was not until 1913 that his first really major cinema opened in New York and it was designed by Lamb. Called the Regent Theatre, it was sited in Harlem on Seventh Avenue at its junction with 116th Street, but failed initially to capitalise on either its size or the richness of its interior decoration. However, by 1914 a man named Samuel Lionel Rothapfel (nicknamed and today almost only remembered as 'Roxy') had arrived in New York and had become its manager, and by his showmanship began transforming the Regent. He was a man who had begun in early 1908 by opening a 'theatre' room at the rear of a tavern in a small mining town in Pennsylvania. He was then 25 years old and his constant quest after new gimmicks, and his wish to improve the quality of entertainment through films, soon led him to New York. He moved on in 1914 to the newly completed Strand Theatre on 47th Street and Broadway, which was Thomas Lamb's second vast movie palace. This was undoubtedly the grandest and most spectacular cinema yet built, and was described as having 'gilt and marble and deep pile rugs, crystal chandeliers hanging from the ceiling and original art works on the walls, with luxurious lounges and comfortable chairs, a thirty-piece symphony orchestra and a mighty Wurlitzer'.

Roxy was becoming established as the world's greatest showman, and he and Thomas Lamb went on in New York in 1916 to rebuild Hammerstein's Music Hall on 42nd Street and Broadway as the Rialto, and then to design the new Rivoli Theatre on Broadway in 1917. The Rialto was called the 'Temple of the Motion Picture' and the Rivoli the 'Triumph of the Motion Picture'. Roxy was above all of course a marvellous self-publicist, but his great skills as theatre manager, impresario and interior designer were undeniable, and he also launched the highly successful career of Thomas W. Lamb.

Lamb, who was born in Dundee and whose family emigrated to the United States when he was twelve years old, rapidly became established as the most sought-after of American cinema designers. He was, as Ben Hall has described him in *The Best Remaining Seats*, 'the first major

*Above* The Roxy, New York, by Walter W. Ahlschlager, 1927. The 6200 seat 'Cathedral of Motion Pictures'. Demolished in 1961

*Right* A typical 'dream palace' of the early twenties. The Coliseum Theatre, Seattle

architect to make his name in movie theatres'. He showed considerable understanding of neo-classical motifs, and freely adapted 18th-century Adam detailing with a good deal of consistency and sensitivity. However he was most at home interpreting the designs of the French Empire period. In particular he almost invariably treated the exteriors of his buildings classically, with lavish use of faience tiling simulating stone.

By the early twenties, cinemas were becoming bigger and bigger. Lamb's Capitol Theatre on Broadway opened in 1919 and was taken over by Roxy. It seated 5300 and before demolition was the grandest yet with its profusion of gold leaf and crystal chandeliers. By 1921 Lamb had been responsible for the design of over 300 cinemas, a remarkable output in the short space of twelve years. Apart from John Eberson, the other major American cinema architects of the era mostly followed in Lamb's classical footsteps, although frequently veering towards more baroque extravagance and vulgarity than Lamb would ever have permitted himself. There was William Lee Woollett, who designed Grauman's Metropolitan in Los Angeles in 1923 (which subsequently became the Paramount and was pulled down long ago) and P. Thornton Mayre, Alger and Vinour who did the Fox in Atlanta, Georgia in 1929. Peery's Egyptian Theatre in Ogden, Utah was derived from Grauman's Egyptian of two years earlier;

it was designed in 1924 by Leslie S. Hodgson and Myrl A. McClenahan. The somewhat unfortunately named Herbert J. Krapp designed the Jackson in Jackson Heights, Queens, New York City in 1926.

The first so-called, 'moderne' cinema was the San Mateo in San Mateo, California, designed in 1925 by Morrow and Garren. It was, however, a fairly isolated example, and most others followed in the Lamb tradition like Saenger's in New Orleans (Emile Weil, 1928); The Warner Atlantic City, New Jersey (Hoffman-Henon, 1929); and the Fox Arlington in Santa Barbara, California (Edwards and Plunkett, 1931). More exotic were the Egyptian theatres in Boise, Idaho (1927) by Tourtellotte and Hummel, and Boston (1929) by Eisenberg and Feer; and the Mayan in Los Angeles (1927) by Morgan, Walls and Clements. A stunning example of art deco is to be found at the Paramount, Oakland, California, designed in 1931 by Timothy Pfleuger, and beautifully restored in the early 1970s.

C. Howard Crane is particularly interesting because he designed one cinema in London later in his career. He began in 1914 with the Liberty in Detroit, and other prominent cinemas were the Grand, Pittsburgh (1920), the Allen, Cleveland (1921), the Fox, Detroit (1928), and the Fox, St. Louis (1929). It was not until 1937 that he designed the vast Gaumont (now Odeon) in London's Holloway, hardly an elegant building, but with more than a touch of transatlantic panache about it.

Walter W. Ahlschlager was a Chicago architect whose career began about 1920. His first major cinema theatre, the Senate at the junction of Madison and Kedzie Avenues in Chicago, opened in February 1921. It was demolished as recently as January 1977 in the continuing tide of closure and loss of the great American movie palaces. In 1927 he was responsible for what was to be the largest, most expensive, and visually most sensational of all movie palaces: the Roxy at 7th Avenue and 50th Street in New York, for the same movie mogul who was Thomas Lamb's patron. Its scale and its magnificence proved a touchstone for cinema designers and it cost twelve million dollars to build. The interior in fact was planned and decorated along relatively conventional classical theatrical lines by Harold Rambusch, but with an initial vast seating capacity of 6200, subsequently reduced to 5800. Samuel Rothapfel had at last overstepped the mark in his prodigious ego-trip. Unlike Britain, where the super cinema boom was only to begin with the advent of the talkies, in America promoters in 1927 were already worrying about the financial stability of the motion picture industry before Al Jolson's *The Jazz Singer* even hit the screens. The Roxy, New York was destined not to survive, in spite of its vast expense, on account of its sheer size and inflexibility. It was demolished in 1961, but it is to Paul Morand in his book *New York* that we owe the most authentic evocation of the Roxy in its heyday:

Enter this temple of Solomon . . . the brazen doors of the Ark of the Covenant open into a hall with golden cupolas, in old style, and a ceiling with storied panels. Satan has hung this disused sanctuary with scarlet velvet; a nightmare light falls from bowls of imitation alabaster; from yellow glass lanterns, from branching ritual candlesticks: the organ pipes, lit from beneath by greenish lights, make one think of a cathedral under the waves, and in the walls are niches awaiting sinful bishops. I find a seat in a deep, soft fauteuil, from which for two hours I witness giant kisses on mouths like the crevasses of the Grand Canyon, embraces of titans, a whole propaganda of the flesh which maddens, without satisfying, these violent American temperaments. It is more than a Black Mass; it is a profanation of everything . . . I vow I had there a complete vision of the end of the world. I saw Broadway suddenly as one vast Roxy, one of those unsubstantial treasures, one of those joy-baited traps, one of those fleeting and illusory gifts won by the spells of wicked magicians.

In those few sentences, in prose almost worthy of Scott Fitzgerald, Morand has conjured up the whole essence of the cinema as an experience and an escape from the realities of life outside.

Roxy's own description for his creation was the 'Cathedral of Motion Pictures', but the cracks were appearing in the edifices of showmanship and unlimited expense. Walter Ahlschlager went on in 1929 to design, also in New York, the Beacon Theatre. In the event, the Beacon, on Broadway and 74th Street, proved to be one of the last movie palaces built before the Depression, and unlike so many others of the 'hard-top' variety, it has recently been sumptuously restored to something like its former opulence. Barry R. Kerr, one of the entrepreneurs who paid for the restoration, recalled that 'when we first walked into this theater, I just fell down and said "My God, I can't believe this place"'.

The Beacon was originally intended to be the first of a chain of satellite Roxy cinemas throughout New York City, and opened on Christmas Eve 1929 with *Tiger Rose* starring Lupe Velez and Rin Tin Tin, and was described as 'a bit of Baghdad on Upper Broadway', a comment which might just as well have been applied to the film. Unlike the more purist classical approach of Thomas Lamb, the eclectic Ahlschlager mixed his styles and details with abandon. At the Beacon, arguably the finest surviving New York cinema, there are Persian frescoes, Egyptian sphinxes, Roman shields and helmets, 1000 bulb Venetian glass chandeliers and other light fittings, gigantic Greek Urns, Byzantine and Aztec designs, as well as two colossal gilded statues of Britannia flanking and guarding the proscenium arch. As if that were not enough, the magnificent original mighty Wurlitzer has also been restored: 19 ranks and four manuals, complete with special effects right down to the klaxon of an old Ford car.

C. W. and George L. Rapp were as prolific cinema designers as Thomas Lamb, and lacked nothing of his flair for dramatic effect within their invariably adopted classical idiom. After their early start in 1909–10, they were never short of work until the Depression. In 1917 they designed the splendid Central Park cinema in Chicago, with seating under a vast dome painted with murals in the 18th-century manner. Although since remodelled as a church, it survives substantially intact. In succeeding years, they designed the Palace in Chicago; the Capitol on Broadway (1919); the Tivoli, Chicago (1920, demolished), Ruben's Rialto Square in Joliet, Illinois (1926); The Paramount Toledo Theatre in Toledo, Ohio (1928); the Ambassador in St Louis (1928); and the Paramount in Brooklyn (1928). Their Loew's Kings Theatre in Brooklyn (1929) was the first American cinema to open specially designed for talkies. Their greatest achievement was the spectacular Paramount in New York City in 1926, not least because it occupied the lower part of a skyscraper 450 feet high in Times Square. The cinema interior was gutted and destroyed in 1964. Later came the New Southtown (1931) and the Will Rogers (1936) both in Chicago.

Before passing to John Eberson and the atmospherics, a word should

Central Park cinema, Chicago, 1917 by C. W. and George L. Rapp. Now a church

be said about Thomas Lamb's career in the twenties and the influence he and the classical 'hard-top' school had upon British cinema architecture. Many of the movie palaces already mentioned have disappeared or been mutilated beyond recall, and Lamb's output is no exception. In 1921 he designed Loew's State on 45th Street and Broadway, and the next year Loew's Theatre on Gates Avenue and Broadway opened. Also in 1922 Lamb designed the Fox in Philadelphia for William Fox, one of the most important cinema showmen with a national chain. In 1923 the Ambassador in Washington, DC opened, and in 1928 Loew's Ohio Theatre in Columbus, Ohio. The same year saw the Albee in Cincinnati open, a celebrated movie palace that was demolished as recently as April 1977.

Two more cinemas followed in 1929 designed for the great entrepreneur Marcus Loew, the State in Syracuse and the Pitkin in Brooklyn, which was an atmospheric decorated in 'Hispano-Moresque' style, to quote contemporary publicity. But it was also in 1929 that the Fox in San Francisco was designed by Lamb, and it marked the apotheosis before the crash of the Depression. William Fox, of course, sought above all to outdo his rivals, and the final result was dubbed the 'Fabulous and Foolish Fox'. It was not as large as the New York Roxy, but it was the most spectacular movie palace on the West Coast, and no expense was spared by way of

Precursor of recent cinemas in Britain? The Paramount Theatre in New York (1926) by C. W. and George L. Rapp occupies the bottom part of a skyscraper

sumptuous plasterwork and ornate gilded decoration. It has been alleged, with more than a touch of malice, that much of the internal vulgarity and excess was due to Mrs William Fox who liked to advise on the décor of her husband's cinemas, and who, no doubt, hastened his downfall by over-expenditure. Seating 5000 and costing five million dollars to construct, it was doomed to failure as the economy began to crumble just before the Depression. Within three years, William Fox was bankrupt and the pinnacle of his empire had closed to the public. It was the last fanfare to the age of traditional theatres blown up to super cinema proportions, a riot of fibrous plasterwork that was to prove as insubstantial as the material itself.

Thomas Lamb continued designing cinemas in the thirties, principally Loew's 175th Street Theatre and the Mayfair, both in New York in 1930; the Fox at Hackensack, New Jersey (1931); the Lake at Oak Park, Illinois (1936); and the Lincoln at Miami Beach, Florida (also 1936, which he designed in association with Herbert E. Collins).

In the earlier twenties in Britain, most of the significant cinema architects such as Frank Verity and Robert Atkinson were clearly indebted to Thomas Lamb and the traditional school of design, but they added little to what had already been produced, and they were operating within much more modest proportions and scale. Until the first real atmospherics appeared in Britain in 1929, most designers were content to adopt the classical theatre-inspired mould, and nowhere does this view find better amplification and support than in the writings of P. Morton Shand. Although he was not an architect, his *Modern Theatres and Cinemas*, published in 1930, was influential in demonstrating his allegiance to the Modern Movement, and the consequent rectitude of cinema design on the Continent, especially in Germany. He approved of the Lamb school because it was architecturally 'solid' and correct, he abhorred the atmospherics, calling them 'this nauseating stick-jaw candy, so fulsomely flavoured with the syrupy romanticism of popular novels and the "see Naples and die" herd-nostalgia which speeds Cook's conducted tours on their weary ways'. This was of course arrogant and patronising nonsense, but it also totally escaped him that cinema audiences were naturally going to respond most favourably to the most colourful escapist fantasy that could be devised by way of cinema decoration. They were hardly likely to be impressed or moved if the influence of Le Corbusier were to find its way into the cinema auditorium. It reads as something of a contradiction elsewhere in the book when Morton Shand assures us that 'we want to be amused and not instructed, intrigued but not edified. The pedagogue was never more unpopular. Culture must wear her laurels not only lightly, but jauntily'. Thus a true pedagogue condemns himself and provides the perfect justification and introduction to the work of John Eberson.

John Eberson has remained largely unknown outside America as an architect, except to a few cinema building enthusiasts. He emigrated to the United States in 1901 from Austria, having been educated in Dresden, and at the University of Vienna, where he concentrated on technical engineering. His first American employment was with an electrical contractor in St Louis, where he soon became involved in cinema and theatre design following the successful installation of electrical apparatus in a new theatre at Vicksburg, Mississippi. In 1908 he set up his own architectural office (though he never had formal architectural training) at Hamilton, Ohio. Two years later his burgeoning practice and experience necessitated a move to Chicago, where his work continued successfully, if modestly, until the boom in 'movie madness' suddenly made his fortune, for, using his electrical engineering background, he was able to produce a totally new solution for his many commissions. In fact he is known to have designed over 500 cinemas during his career.

His technological innovation, for that is how it must be described, was the 'atmospheric'. As a reaction to the vast expense of erecting a glittering new movie palace full of sumptuous gilded plasterwork, Eberson invented the ingenious lighting effects and stage set decorations that earned him the title of 'Father of the Atmospheric Theatre'. The lighting effects were predominantly stars and clouds; the stage sets consisted of exotic outdoor locations arranged around the auditorium walls and proscenium arch. Not only did this type of interior provide a welcome contrast and alternative to the Thomas Lamb formal academic school, it also had the inestimable benefit of being far cheaper to build and maintain. It is calculated that on average an Eberson atmospheric cost approximately one quarter of the total of a comparable Lamb model. The biggest saving was in the ceiling, where a simple plaster vault with lighting effects could suffice in place of all the gilded cornices, domes and other plaster mouldings, not to mention the crystal chandeliers. The special effects were simply produced, the twinkling stars were low wattage bulbs operating as small circuits in sequence, and the clouds were created by revolving gauze discs illuminated by a magic lantern.

Even Thomas Lamb capitulated to some extent to his new rival, for he wrote that the atmospheric 'would retain its novelty character for a considerable length of time'. Faced with their ability to attract at least as great crowds as his own cinemas, Lamb even designed, no doubt half-heartedly, a few atmospherics of his own, including Loew's Pitkin Theatre in Brooklyn, already referred to, and Loew's 72nd Street Theatre in New York in 1932, where Lamb's classical exterior had an atmospheric interior by Eberson.

Above all, Eberson's greatest success was in the vital area of ensuring complete client satisfaction. His office slogan was 'Prepare Practical Plans for Pretty Playhouses – Please Patrons – Pay Profits', and he experimented constantly with methods of lowering operating costs for his clients. To this end he established Michelangelo Studios, a company specialising in the designing and mass production of his special effects. The studio then contracted its services and supervised the construction of each cinema, thus ensuring the creation of low-priced but expensive-looking interiors, and also maintaining the quality of workmanship involved. Major design elements were used again and again, but always ingeniously disguised. Thus the proscenium arch in Richmond, Virginia also appeared in Detroit, the statuary in Houston's Italian garden re-appeared in Tampa's Spanish courtyard, and so on. Every Eberson interior was a triumph of design, invention and lighting, none of them historically accurate, but most sought the Mediterranean countries for their inspiration, and as far as most of the patrons knew, they were true to life. As Eberson himself remarked, each of his theatres aimed for 'an aura of realistic enchantment'.

Eberson used colour to its fullest extent, and indeed liked the name 'colourist' to be applied to himself and his associates. Three quotations from an article he wrote in 1927 perhaps sum up best in his own words what he was trying to achieve.

We visualize and dream a magnificent amphitheatre under a glorious moonlit sky in an Italian garden, in a Persian court, in a Spanish patio, or in a mystic Egyptian temple-yard, all canopied by a soft moonlit sky.

One of the great John Eberson atmospherics. The Italian Gardens in the Capitol Theatre, Chicago (1926)

We credit the deep azure blue of the Mediterranean sky with a therapeutic value, soothing the nerves and calming perturbing thoughts.

The very nature of the pastel colouring executed in hundreds of desired shades and colours, lends itself so well to the imagination of the average person, and as we linger and look about, our fancy is free to conjure endless tales of romance.

John Eberson's first atmospherics were completed in 1923: the Orpheum, Wichita and, much more important, the Majestic, Houston, which created the effect of an Italian Renaissance garden. By the end of the twenties, he had designed nearly a hundred atmospherics including such masterpieces as the Capitol (another Italian garden) and Paradise (1928, demolished 1954) in Chicago; the Riviera in Omaha (yet another Italian garden designed to rival the 2700 seat Orpheum and the Paramount at Cedar Rapids); the Riviera, Detroit; the Olympia, Miami (1926, now the Gusman Center); the Tampa, Florida (a Spanish courtyard); the State, Kalamazoo (1927); the Palace, Marion, Ohio (1928); and the Majestic, San Antonio (1929). The Avalon, Chicago (1927) became a Miracle Temple in 1970 and in Tampa the city have taken over the cinema and made a good job of restoring it.

However, Eberson's greatest source of fame was to come from Marcus Loew, head of the Loew's Theatre Corporation, and yet another of the legendary cinema entrepreneurs of America's golden age of film. John Eberson created his most celebrated atmospheric for Marcus Loew in 1926, the Paradise Theatre in the Bronx, New York. Many of the amazing effects in this cinema were achieved by means of *trompe-l'oeil* painting, and altogether it was a triumph of rococo Italianate decoration. Today it stands tripled, mutilated and neglected. Hardly less impressive was the

Loew's in Richmond, Virginia. Such was the anticipation of the opening of this cinema in April 1928, that the local *Times-Dispatch* newspaper commented: 'Imagine years of planning for this magnificent new show-place. Imagine all the luxury, comfort, and dazzling beauty of color and ornamentation that you ever dreamed of in a theatre and you're still miles shy of what you're going to see in the new Loew's Theatre'. It continued that Loew's was 'appointed in a manner suggestive of a Spanish Castle of the first order', and 'it has always been suspected that the theatre to most persons is a refuge from reality. But, until recently the illusion was confined to the entertainment presented there. Now the purpose is to surround the patron with this illusion, to swaddle him with luxury'.

One of the earliest British atmospherics. The Richmond cinema (now the Odeon) by Leathart and Granger (1929)

On 9 April 1928, Loew's, Richmond opened its doors to an eager public, and greeted them with ushers 'dressed in the splendor of Bulgarian Generals'. A musical programme centred on 'Wild Oscar at the organ', who was also 'a deft exponent of syncopation, a nimble musical trickster and a singer of pleasant and agreeable voice'. There was also the movie, a silent entitled *West Point*, and Loew's trademark, parrots, of which there were four stuffed and two live! White doves flew in and around the alcoves on the sides of the auditorium and altogether his client and public could certainly not have been disappointed by Eberson's achievements. The last great American movie palace was Radio City Music Hall, opened in 1932 and designed by Donald Deskey to seat 5960; it remains a triumph of ostentacious, if coarse, art-deco design. Before passing to the London Astorias, mention must be made of the two celebrated Grauman's cinemas in Hollywood, California, designed by Meyer and Holler. Although they were not widely influential in America, they made their impact in England, and George Coles, in particular, was much influenced by them. Grauman's Egyptian was

The auditorium of the Richmond cinema

Details from the Richmond cinema: doors and a frieze

designed in 1922, and Grauman's Chinese in 1927. Grauman's Egyptian seems to have been particularly startling in its efforts to outdo even Tutankhamun. As Ben Hall remarks in *The Best Remaining Seats*, it 'made King Tut's tomb look like the old family burial vault'. It was at Grauman's Chinese that contemporary stars of the silver screen developed the habit of literally leaving their footprint for posterity.

The first real atmospheric to appear in Britain was probably the Richmond cinema (now tripled as an Odeon), designed in 1929 by Julian Leathart and W. F. Granger. The auditorium was designed to simulate a Spanish courtyard and garden, and £10 000 was spent on an elaborate colour-change lighting installation. This enormously expensive interior represented a change in direction for Leathart and Granger, all the more surprising since Leathart had rather sarcastically dubbed atmospherics on one occasion as 'outside-in' interiors. It also brought down on their heads the wrath of P. Morton Shand, who accused Leathart of 'going over to the enemy in his new cinema at Richmond', and producing an interior of 'architecturalised acoustics'.

However, by far the most important group of early London atmospherics were the four London Astoria cinemas built for Paramount and designed by Edward A. Stone, later of the well-known architectural practice of Stone, Toms and Partners, with interior decoration by Tommy Somerford and Ewen Barr. T. R. (Tommy) Somerford, who died in June 1948, is otherwise best known as the architect for Temperance Billiard Halls Ltd, and he designed many of the early halls to be seen around London. Ewen Barr designed the Duchess Theatre in London. These movie palaces were the true English successors to the American atmospherics and very much in the same tradition, all being provided with full stage facilities. The first of them was completed late in 1929 on a big, roughly triangular, corner site in Stockwell Road, Brixton. Publicity for

The Astoria, Brixton, first of the major atmospherics in London

the cinema boasted that it was designed to hold 4500 people, making it the biggest cinema at that time in Britain. In the event compliance with means of escape requirements dictated a maximum seating capacity of 2982. It dominates the townscape in crude fashion and cannot be regarded as an asset in any view with its small copper-domed corner entrance overshadowed by the bulk of what seems like several acres of fletton walling. The auditorium is on the open forum plan, with Italianate garden scenes around the walls. To quote Ian Cameron (in the *Sunday Times* Magazine 1965), the patrons 'could look down at the monumental doorways and pergolas dripping with plaster vines, ahead to a flattened miniature of the rialto along the top of the proscenium arch, sideways to the walls topped with statues under the Lombardy poplars, seen against the sky'. Formerly the Rialto Bridge proscenium arch had figures moving across it to complete the effect, and it was here that the opening publicity coined the phrase 'An Acre of Seats in a Garden of Dreams'. The future of the Astoria has been in doubt since it closed in January 1973 and much of the plasterwork has since been mutilated. Successive plans to turn the cinema into a warehouse and a skateboard rink have failed in spite of Rank's sympathetic attitude towards the building. A venture as a popular music venue was also short lived, and the most likely future use now seems to be as an indoor market.

The Streatham Astoria (1930), designed by Edward A. Stone. The only elegant exterior among the London Astoria group

The second Astoria to open was in the Old Kent Road. Marginally smaller than Brixton, but larger than the other two, it has an indifferent exterior, but an interesting and beautiful semi-atmospheric interior using art deco motifs. It was never situated in a very commercial position and closed in 1968, though it still stands, and was briefly used in 1978–9 as a skateboard rink.

Fountain court at the Astoria,
Finsbury Park. Some of the
qualities of a Moorish harem
caught in this interior (1930)
by Tommy Somerford and
Ewen Barr

A detail from the Astoria,
Finsbury Park. Signs of the
excessive wear and tear
generated by use for pop
concerts can be seen top right

Third to open was the Astoria, Streatham, now the Odeon, and this has a far more ambitious exterior with a monumental entrance façade in a hybrid Italianate style, beautifully constructed in brick with stone dressings. The striking interior, which was strongly Egyptian in atmospheric character, and had a stage larger than Drury Lane, was mercilessly swept away in a reconstruction in 1962 and the auditorium has since been further altered.

Last of the quartet in 1930 was the Astoria, Finsbury Park, still the best preserved and most loved of the group. As at Brixton, it occupies a large corner site in an ungainly fashion with an extremely clumsy corner entrance, but once inside the planning is ingenious. An evocative description came from Deyan Sudjic (*Building Design* 1 February 1974):

You are greeted by the illuminated fountain of a Moorish harem, complete with goldfish. Above, the building rises to the circle lounge, domed with a Byzantine cupola. It's as if the architect had flicked through his Banister Fletcher and recreated in plaster all the illustrations that caught his fancy.

Throughout there's a fantastic mix of all the most exotic historical styles. The mirrors come from the Baroque. The wall friezes from Bengal. But when you get into the auditorium you realise there's more to it than mere historical recreation. In the corners of the hall, hanging above the brick Romanesque proscenium are tropical villages, disappearing to hills on the horizon.

Apart from the Granada, Tooting, there is no more striking cinema interior in Britain than this, with its Moorish city crowding around the proscenium arch guarded by towers and gilded lions. In a sense, also, its new life in the seventies as a venue for rock concerts seems curiously appropriate.

With the Finsbury Park Astoria, atmospherics had arrived in England with a flair never to be repeated, and the 1930s had been ushered in towards a new era of super cinemas.

# 5

# THE TALKIES AND THE SUPERS

Too much stylishness makes an unkind frame for a scene or picture that will most often have no stylishness at all.

GOODHART-RENDEL on cinema design, 1937

British Picture houses need a drastic 'Pride's Purge' to free them from the clogging dross of period reproduction and that craving for mere gaudiness that still strangles original design.

P. MORTON SHAND, 1930

N 1928 the 'talkies' arrived in Britain, a new word for a new experience. Technically it was not a new idea, as experiments had been carried out in combining pictures with sound and music almost before the film industry had begun. In Edison's laboratory an early peep-show machine had been linked to a phonograph in 1888. The first inventor to patent a Talkie Film machine was Eugène Lauste who combined Frieze-Green's projection equipment with the results of sound experiments by a German scientist called Ruhmer. In 1906 Lauste exhibited films with a sound track that operated a photo-electric cell in the projector. By all accounts, these were a success and they formed the basis for all the later experiments and developments. However, Lauste's patents lapsed and he did not live to see his ideas become commercially profitable, but after his death in 1925, his ideas and machines were extensively copied by the film corporations.

As early as 1907 in London there had been an experimental showing of films accompanied by sound to a fee-paying public. This was a 16-week season at the London Hippodrome in Charing Cross Road where recordings of Harry Lauder's voice were synchronised to films in which he was acting. It was as the promoters called it, 'the illusion of life', and where he could be seen singing on the screen, his voice was reproduced by talking machines through a chronophone. Two of the earliest systems of a basic type of sound and film synchronisation were Barker's Cinephone and Cecil Hepworth's Vivaphone. Gaumont had first tried out a system in 1902, which they improved in 1910, but their main problem proved to be distortion of sound through the auditorium loudspeakers.

*On previous page* The auditorium of the Forum in Liverpool. A superbly composed impression of monumental scale within a quite modest space

The talkies arrive: queuing in Birmingham at the West End cinema in 1929

It was Warner Brothers who first exploited the commercial possibilities of sound when they decided in 1925 to produce sound on disc films. They used a silent film *Don Juan* first, for which they recorded a musical accompaniment. Then in 1927 they decided to make the first film with the Vitaphone system where words and music formed an integral part of the actual story. The result was Al Jolson in *The Jazz Singer*, closely followed by *The Singing Fool*, and in 1929 over 300 cinemas were being planned or built in Britain to cope with the new phenomenon. For example, the ABC circuit was formed with 40 halls, which figure had grown to 160 within two years.

These cinemas became known as the 'supers', not a name that specifically referred only to cinemas built after the advent of sound, but nevertheless one that conveniently describes the new, even larger and more elaborate cinemas that began to mushroom everywhere from 1929 onwards. 1929 had seen the launching of the celebrated London Astoria chain, not only the first co-ordinated attempt at a corporate house style or image, but also representing the first influx of American style atmospherics. The thirties, and the super cinemas that the period generated, also made the reputation of several important architects who might otherwise have passed their careers almost unnoticed, but for 'movie madness'. The finest of the supers are probably best described under the architects who created them, starting with E. Wamsley Lewis and the New Victoria in Wilton Road, Westminster.

As a work of architecture there is little doubt that the New Victoria is the most important cinema building to have been erected in Britain. As has so often occurred in the creation of masterpieces, Ernest Wamsley Lewis happened to be in the right place at the right time, and he was able to produce the only truly international cinema of the thirties, apart perhaps from the original Curzon in Mayfair. When Wamsley Lewis joined the AA school in 1920, the revolt against the use of the classical orders on steel or reinforced concrete buildings was under way. As Wamsley Lewis wrote in *London Architect* in January 1972, 'Robert Atkinson was our headmaster, succeeded by Howard Robertson'. Few public buildings in the twenties were approved by the rising young stars of the architectural profession and the only really respected practices seem to have been Sir John Burnet, Tait and Lorne, and Sylvester Sullivan. But European influence was growing: there was Kramer and, more especially, Dudok and Berlage in Holland, and the brick forms of Dudok were to find much favour among British architects in the thirties.

Wamsley Lewis was already interested in theatre design. Immediately after the First World War, he had visited Prague and Berlin, seen the work of Otto Wagner in Vienna, and been much influenced by Auguste Perret's Théâtre des Champs-Elysées in Paris. In 1927 Lewis won the Bossom scholarship for the study of theatres. He went to Germany to examine stage mechanism and lighting, and the psychology of colour, and the planning of his competition design was based on the teaching of Robert Atkinson and his Regent cinema in Brighton and also W. H. Watkins, architect of the Regent cinema, Bristol. Lewis went on to America to study the architecture of the theatre, and worked for some time in the office of C. Howard Crane. While he was there, the Ziegfeld Theatre in New York opened, and its architect Joseph Urban invited Lewis to work with him on the design of the new Metropolitan Opera House, but Urban died and Lewis returned to England after nine months.

Soon after his return he was called to the office of William Evans, Managing Director of Provincial Cinematograph Theatres and invited to design a new super cinema on a site in Victoria with a budget of a quarter of a million pounds. And so the New Victoria was born. E. Wamsley Lewis has written extensively of the influences that were brought to bear in his design: there was the Skandia Cinema in Stockholm by Asplund, several theatres in Berlin by Oskar Kaufmann (especially in their use and treatment of wood panelling), the Universum Cinema in Berlin by Erich Mendelsohn in the way lighting was used, and the external treatment of the Titania Palast. But most of all there was the Grosses Schauspielhaus in Berlin, designed by Hans Poelzig in 1919. It was this auditorium with its masses of stalactites suspended from the arched roof and controlled coloured lighting effects that were the primary influence in the creation of

The Grosses Schauspielhaus in Berlin, designed by Hans Poelzig in 1919. The inspiration for the New Victoria cinema

the underwater palace effects in the New Victoria. Technically the lighting effects were to be the most ambitious ever attempted in an English cinema, and their sophistication was largely due to Lewis's studies with the stage lighting director at the Dresden Opera House.

W. E. Trent, the architect to Provincial Cinematograph Theatres, to whom the New Victoria has usually been ascribed in the past, had no more part in the design than the executive control of finances, and Lewis had to obtain his authority for spending the budget. Apart from this, Trent evidently let Lewis get on with it, in conjunction with his client William Evans. The New Victoria is a triumph first and foremost of ingenious and compact planning on a very cramped and awkward site that had the disadvantage of having two principal road frontages, each of which was required to be a main entrance. These two exterior elevations are quite unlike any other cinema ever built in England, with their vigorous vertical entrance bays contrasted with the long horizontal banding of the auditorium walls all carried out in artificial stone. For the time of building in 1929/30, this was one of the earliest and boldest expressions of the Continental influence in Britain, and it was far nearer the International Modern Movement than any cinema before or since, although Erich Mendelsohn and the functionalist architects are the closest point of contact.

The interior is an amalgam of atmospheric effects and carefully developed art deco designs and motifs adding up to the desired impression of a fairy-tale 'Mermaid's Palace'. Many of these decorative features had a purely practical purpose, but they all contributed to the overall underwater palace effect. The acoustics were designed by Hope Bagenal, and the surfaces of the great auditorium dome were broken up by the individual application, by hand, of some 40,000 fibrous plaster hemispheres, each the size of half a tennis ball. The various sculptured panels in pure art deco manner were executed by Newberry Trent, a cousin of W. E. Trent, and made in a French concrete material called Lap. The colour

The auditorium of the New Victoria photographed at its opening in 1930. Little has changed apart from the removal of the stalactite lights

scheme and the colours of the lighting effects were of the greatest importance. Lewis recalls how the day before the opening he thought the colours of some bulbs were wrong, so he and the engineer personally changed some 3000 bulbs from the access catwalks, starting at 3 am in the morning! The interior still creates a remarkable effect, even with the removal of the original stalactite light fittings and the changing of the original cool blue and green colours to the present scheme of gold and autumnal tints. It is no longer a Mermaid's Palace, and although not by any means the earliest super cinema in Britain, it remains one of the most exciting. What is equally remarkable is that the final cost of the building worked out at £89,000 not £250,000 as budgeted, and how often does that happen today?

E. Wamsley Lewis recalls that when the building was going up, the windowless walls induced the reaction of calls of 'Sing Sing' from passing bus conductors, and the London *Evening News* referred to it as 'that

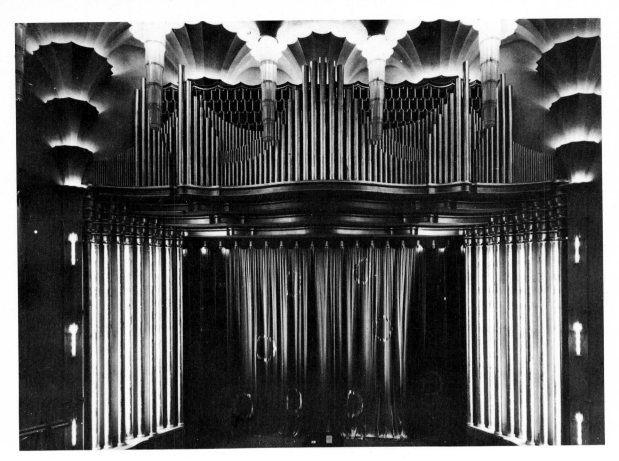

Another 1930 photograph of the proscenium of the New Victoria. The very spirit of art deco

Juggernaut'. An article by Arnold Bennett in *The Times* on 'Revolt in Architecture' illustrated the New Victoria as one of his examples. Sidney Bernstein, of Granada fame, remarked to Lewis on the opening night in October 1930 that 'people do not want this sort of thing: they want architecture with marble columns, gilt and mirrors. This won't pay'. He may have been right, but the New Victoria has always been a great success in all but its geographic location, which, in spite of its proximity to a major London railway terminal, seems to have militated against its use as a 'showcase' cinema. The recent history of the New Victoria has been far from happy. In spite of statutory listing by the Government, the building closed in 1976 and negotiations have continued over several possible future uses, mainly concerned with the extent of alterations required for a cabaret club or discothèque use. It is a particularly regrettable state of affairs following a long period when the Rank Organisation seemed bent on hastening the end of the New Victoria by their policy of only showing, on a week-by-week basis, double bills of films of the sort not shown to critics and guaranteed to empty any 2400 seat auditorium. The stage, of good size, and full dressing room facilities might have been the salvation of the building had the Festival Ballet, who had enjoyed two seasons a year in the cinema for some time, been able to afford to extend their activities on a more permanent basis. Instead a short-lived experi-

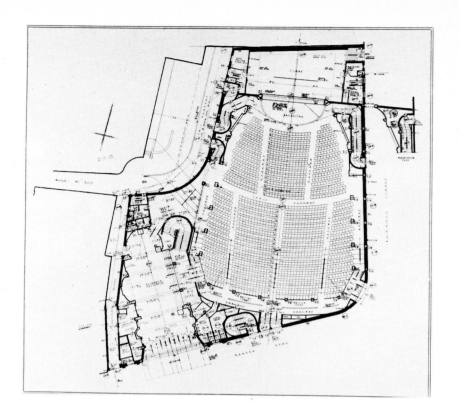

ment with pop concerts failed, although it has now re-opened for pop concerts, renamed the Apollo Victoria. It was to be the cinema's loss that shortly
after completion of the New Victoria, E. Wamsley Lewis decided to leave
London and settle on the south coast where he set up his own quietly
successful private practice. He never designed another super cinema.

Since W. E. Trent enjoyed an executive function in relation to the
New Victoria, but was himself responsible for many fine cinemas elsewhere, it is appropriate to consider his contribution next. William Edward
Trent, FSI began designing Gaumonts in 1921 at East Ham; and all were
distinguished by their brilliant planning, often the solutions encom-
passing difficult or extremely cramped site conditions. In 1928 the first of
a chain of large super cinemas opened, built by Provincial Cinematograph
Theatres and designed by Trent. It was the Regent cinema (now tripled)
in Upwell Street, Sheffield, and it was typical of much that he did later. It
seated 2300, had a café restaurant with accommodation for 150 diners, a
full stage with dressing room facilities, and a good size orchestra pit with
electric organ console. The plan was in Trent's favourite fan shape and the
decorations were intended to create the illusion of an Italian palace, with a
great double dome in the auditorium, and a mexxanine crush-hall
designed like the loggia of the palace with open balustrades giving views
of murals depicting Italianate gardens. There was also the Gaumont
Palace (now Odeon) in Salisbury, which opened on 7 September 1931,
and utilised the half-timbered house and great hall of a local and
prosperous 15th-century wool merchant, John Halle, for the foyer areas.
This approach set the scene for a preposterous, though effective,

auditorium in the form of a vast baronial hall, seating 1687 patrons. The great mock Tudor beamed ceiling is only approached by Jomisarjevsky's Granadas as a 'solid' decorative exercise, and it is gratifying that although tripled, the main part of the auditorium is still intact, and the whole building is listed thanks to 'Ye halle of Johne Halle'.

In 1932 he designed Gaumont Palaces in Wolverhampton (with a strongly horizontal banded elevation, reminiscent of the New Victoria), Cheltenham and Lewisham. This last named cinema, which closed in 1981, with an undistinguished exterior and a much simplified and modernised interior, enjoyed the privilege, with 3000 seats, of being the largest undivided cinema auditorium left in exclusive cinema use in the London area. Further Gaumont Palaces appeared from his office throughout the thirties, none of them memorable. What Trent might have lacked in the final analysis was real design flair in his Gaumont British Corporation cinemas, but it was more than compensated by his excellent planning and restrained classically correct interiors.

There were many architects working on cinemas in the thirties, all of whom deserve notice: Drury and Gomersall, Robert Cromie, E. Norman Bailey, F. E. Bromige, William R. Glen, A. Ernest Shennan, Hurley Robinson, J. Stanley Beard, Blackmore and Sykes, W. T. Benslyn, Kemp and Tasker, David E. Nye, John Alexander and, above all, George Coles. Their main contribution to cinema design was to reverse the trends noted by P. Morton Shand in 1930:

The cinema ought to be one of the types of building most characteristic of our age, if only because our age is identified both with the invention of the cinematograph and the phenomenal expansion of the film industry. Unfortunately, however, in England its design still wearily rings out the changes of already obsolescent theatre models. With the possible exception of Nonconformist chapels, no class of edifice represents quite such a degraded general level of design. But what was true of yesterday need not be true of tomorrow.

George Coles, who died in 1963, was certainly the most versatile as well as one of the most prolific of all cinema architects, designing with equal facility and success whether in the Egyptian style in Islington, the Chinese style in Southall, artdeco Odeons at Woolwich, Balham and Muswell Hill, or straightforward neo-classical at Kilburn. He has a good claim to be considered the most notable and talented of all the major cinema architects, and his practice carried on in his name in Craven Street, London, until the end of 1979. During a long career in cinema design, which began in the early twenties, he worked for every major cinema circuit.

His first great triumph as a cinema architect was in 1927 at the Broadway cinema, Stratford, east London (now a factory), and the following year Coles summed up the reasons for siting super cinemas in suburbs in an article about the Broadway in *Cinemas, Theatres and Ballrooms*.

In the first place, cinemas supply the need of the public for a cheap and attractive form of entertainment reasonably near their homes, to which they can go regularly or at will without any previous booking. It is, therefore, of first importance that the site for such a building should be very carefully considered, not only in regard to its immediate neighbourhood, but also in relation to the surrounding district, as, provided there are good bus or tram services, a super-cinema theatre will draw patrons from an extensive area, and this is of considerable importance to

The Commodore, Stamford Brook (1929). An early George Coles success with a striking atmospheric interior

the success of a house . . . A good frontage to a main road is important, and a dignified façade in such a position cannot fail to attract . . . Much can be done by the correct use of materials to render the entrance façade the attraction it should be, and the use of white glazed terra-cotta has much to recommend it from the point of view of appearance and durability, it is also easily cleaned down, and when floodlighted, has a very festive appearance. The judicious use of black granite, together with terra-cotta, can also be highly recommended. . . . The general decoration of the cinema should be in scale with the size of the building, and be designed so as to lead the eye towards the proscenium opening. Colour decoration may be applied to the walls, providing it does not detract from the lighting effects, for however large the house may be, the general effect when the lights are up, as they frequently are in a super cinema, should be one of warmth and cosiness, rather than that of a cold, vast structure.

The Broadway was a large classically designed building with plenty of marble columns in the foyers and an auditorium lined with arches with illuminated murals of mythical landscapes. In 1928 he designed the Carlton, Upton Park, again in east London, its modest faience façade a sort of 'dummy run' for the Egyptian-style Carlton in Islington that was to follow in a couple of years. It was a 2500 seat cinema planned in the stadium form, which saved it from subdivision, and rather surprisingly this large cinema, with its elegant classical interior is still open, renamed the Ace. Early in 1929 the Commodore Cinema (now closed) at Stamford Brook opened, a large faience-faced cinema, whose bulk, incidentally, wreaked havoc on the beautiful and previously peaceful St Peter's Square behind it. The interior here marked a change in style, for it was of the atmospheric type with murals of gardens and underwater scenes and elaborate lighting effects. P. Morton Shand violently disapproved! 'Another rather interesting recent façade "The Commodore" in Hammersmith is best seen only from without. To enter is to be confronted with an orgy of "atmospherics", every whit as emetic in their reactions as the nougat and Castile soap frescoes of the Brixton "Astoria".'

The Palace, Southall on opening day, 30 November 1929

The Palace today. Still in use as the Liberty: west London's answer to Grauman's Hollywood Chinese

On 30 November 1929 the Palace, Southall opened, surely the most distinctive of all George Coles's cinemas. It is Chinese in style and can only be described as west London's answer to Grauman's Chinese in Hollywood. It is an astonishing building, with its pagoda pantiled roofs, fierce dragon's head finials, and lavish use of coloured faience tiling as fresh today as it was 50 years ago. The interior is also Chinese, but is curiously designed without a circle, not even on a stadium plan. The Palace was designed for United Picture Theatres, who were absorbed by the Gaumont-British circuit in July 1930. The Palace has had a chequered and colourful career; first it became the Gaumont, then the Odeon, then the Godeon (sic) after passing into Asian hands in the early 1970s. Since then it has briefly been the Godina, and is now the Liberty. However, it is

The Egyptian-style Carlton in Islington while still a cinema in 1971. The centre has now been obscured by an insensitive lighting box advertising bingo

still intact inside and out and it was statutorily listed late in 1980 as the unique example of a Chinese-style cinema in Britain.

Next, in 1930, came the almost equally remarkable Carlton in Essex Road, Islington. The front was designed in the Egyptian style, and it remains as a far more assured exercise in the idiom than any of its three other Egyptian rivals in England, the Pyramid at Sale (1933 Drury and Gomersall, later Odeon), the Riviera, Manchester, much altered as a Top Rank bowling rink or the Luxor (now Odeon), Twickenham, by J. Stanley Beard. The Carlton is shades of Karnak indeed, with its bulbous columns, stylised papyrus leaves and pyramidal forms. Again the fluent use of coloured tiling is highly effective, but at the Carlton, George Coles strangely failed to carry the Egyptian style inside into the auditorium. Instead he opted for the safe compromise of neo-classicism of a distinctly French sort. The Carlton, which is statutorily protected, has operated as a bingo club since 1972. Later in 1930 came the Savoy in East Acton and his most colossal London cinema, the literally elephantine Trocadero at the Elephant and Castle. Designed for H. and G. Kinemas Limited (Hyams and Gale), the exterior, uncharacteristically for Coles, was extremely coarse and crudely detailed. However, the interior was a lavish exercise in the Italian Renaissance Style, with much richly detailed plasterwork in the auditorium and full stage facilities, plus a Wurlitzer which alone cost £15,000. The Troc, as it was affectionately known by

The monumental exterior of the Gaumont State, Kilburn, opened in 1937. George Coles's crowning achievement

generations of south Londoners, was demolished in 1966 to make way for a new cinema designed by Erno Goldfinger. Also for H. and G. Kinemas, Coles next altered in 1932 the Trocette in Tower Bridge Road (which had first opened in 1929), recently demolished after lying empty since the early sixties, and in 1933 designed the Troxy in Commercial Road, Stepney. This cinema with a fine front and classical interior, closed in 1960 and became the London Opera Centre.

During the mid and later thirties, Coles was primarily engaged in designing Odeons for Oscar Deutsch and the finest examples in the London area all came from his office. In 1938 he designed his solitary cinema for Granada, at Welling in Kent, a relatively modest effort that is now tripled. But it was in mid-1935 that he began designing (again for H. and G. Kinemas) what was to be perhaps his most spectacular achievement. Taken over by Gaumont-British before it opened, it was the Gaumont State in Kilburn. Opened at the end of 1937, it was described as Coles's crowning achievement, and in terms of size and expense was

The foyer of the Gaumont
State, Kilburn. Tatty modern
counter fittings hardly detract
from the grandeur of the
conception

The splendid Renaissance
interior of the Gaumont State

The Gaumont Palace (now the
Odeon) at Hammersmith
Broadway, London. Robert
Cromie's finest cinema,
opened in 1932

decidedly impressive: 4004 seats at a cost of some £350,000. The exterior is
marked by a tall faience-faced tower, which illuminated at night, dominated the neighbourhood around. The interior is of the richest Renaissance style, owing much to his earlier Trocadero, and also the somewhat
simpler Carlton, Islington. The vast marble-columned foyer and sweeping grand staircase leads to the auditorium, which was, of course, provided with generous full stage facilities. Although listed, this great
cinema, with its equally magnificent Wurlitzer organ is now (1981) closed
and threatened with redevelopment.

After George Coles, Robert Cromie ranks as the cinema architect of
next importance. Much of his work was done for independent cinema
owners or small circuits, and generally speaking his designs can be
categorised as worthy but a little dull and unexciting. Usually they are
distinguished by their flattish, rather square façades with rounded corners, and careful control of detail. Undoubtedly the masterpiece of his
thirties work was the Gaumont Palace (now the Odeon) at Hammersmith
Broadway, a vast building with an enormously wide, gently curving front
façade, now almost completely hidden by the Hammersmith road fly-
over. It was built in 1932, and the detail in brick and artificial stone has
monumental impact. Inside the balcony alone holds some 2000 people,
and it is no surprise to find this cinema finding regular favour as a venue
for rock music concerts. The decorations of the main foyer and
auditorium are strongly art deco in inspiration, and are consistently and
successfully developed, all in all a considerable accomplishment. However, one must remark that the detail owes much both to the Savoy
Theatre in London, and also to Friedrich Lipp's Capitol cinema in Breslau,
with which Cromie presumably was familiar.

The feeling with most of Cromie's work is that his buildings as a
whole hardly add up to the sum of their parts: his redbrick and tiled

A splendid Cromie design for an atmospheric interior; alas unrealised

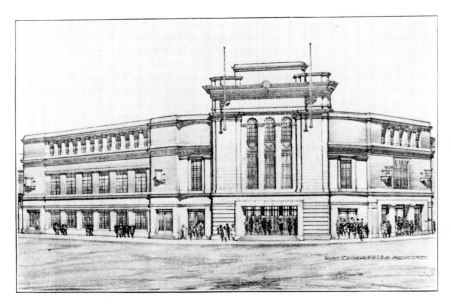

Robert Cromie's original perspective for the Regal (ABC), Beckenham, opened in 1930

façades were rather monotonous, and internally his decorative motifs were almost invariably art deco, used predictably to flank the proscenium arch. His planning was excellent, often making good use of restricted sites. He was very busy during the thirties, designing a great number of Regal and Ritz cinemas, later mostly to become the anonymous ABC cinemas. In 1937 he designed the Prince of Wales Theatre in London's

Coventry Street, a building of quite paralysing dullness. Many of his cinemas have now been demolished and most of the remainder tripled. Perhaps the most typical and attractive examples near London are the ABC Beckenham and the Odeon, Wimbledon both of which have been tripled. The least attractive is undoubtedly the ill-proportioned redbrick cliff of the ABC in Kingston-on-Thames. After the war, Cromie's career fell away somewhat, and he was responsible for an unimaginative internal reconstruction, after war damage, of the Royal Court Theatre in London's Sloane Square in 1952, and later still some office blocks of sadly indeterminate character.

The Regal (Odeon),  . Wimbledon (1933). One of Robert Cromie's most characteristic cinema designs

F. E. Bromige did not design many cinemas, but one, the Grosvenor (later Odeon) in Rayners Lane, Harrow, is a spectacular example of mid-thirties cinema art deco, with a stylised abstract representation in concrete of a curving elephant's trunk as the principal central motif on the front, and a little altered interior that preserves many felicitous details such as original mirrors, light fittings and furniture. Because of the shallow projection of the circle over the stalls, it has never been possible to subdivide the cinema, although a changeover to bingo is a distinct possibility. Other cinemas designed by Bromige in the thirties include the Granada, Hove; the Dominions at Southall, Acton and Harrow; and the Argosy, Sheerness; all displaying a futuristic love of curved glass.

E. Norman Bailey remains a rather obscure figure. From a small office in Maidenhead High Street, E. Norman Bailey and Partners was a practice that enjoyed some success west of London in the thirties. In 1931 he designed the Regal, Uxbridge for Abrahams Consolidated, a building statutorily protected in 1976. Although now closed while discussions continue over its future and possible redevelopment, it is a building that has remained remarkably unchanged, and is one of the most highly

The Regal (ABC),
Kingston-upon-Thames
(1932). A disastrous intrusion
into the townscape

Auditorium of the Odeon,
Rayners Lane (1935).
Unspoiled and curvaceous
cinema art deco

The Grosvenor (Odeon), Rayners Lane, London. F. E. Bromige's totally unexpected art deco masterpiece in a fashionable London dormitory

All the subsidiary fittings of the mid-thirties Odeon in Rayners Lane are intact: a rare and precious survival

The wildly futuristic exterior of F. E. Bromige's Dominion in Harrow. A late 1930s photograph; the exterior survives totally encased in blue sheet material

The unassuming exterior of
the Regal, Uxbridge hides
what is the best art deco
cinema interior in London,
and possibly in Britain

Eccentric, unique and entirely
original detailing on the
auditorium walls of the Regal,
Uxbridge

The extraordinary, almost
Burmese, detailing of doors
at the Regal, Uxbridge

developed exercises in art deco attempted in any cinema, rivalled in
London perhaps only by George Coles's Odeon at Muswell Hill,
designed five years later. Seating 1360, it has, behind a modest façade, a
stadium plan that has once again proved the cinema's salvation from
subdivision. The auditorium ceiling flows in a dazzling sequence of
shaped and scalloped curves and coved fibrous plaster cornices, towards
a uniquely curvaceous proscenium, flanked by plaster panels of Chinese-
influenced decoration. The art deco side doors are so stylised that they
acquire overtones of a Burmese temple, and the remainder of the walls are
treated with an extremely odd assortment of varied but purely art deco
motifs. A two manual Compton organ also survives intact: along with the
Gaumont State, Kilburn, Odeon, Twickenham and Granada, Kingston
one of only four cinema organs in the London area in original condition.

After the Uxbridge Regal, E. Norman Bailey went on to design the
Adelphi in Slough, the Showboat Roadhouse at Maidenhead in 1933, and
the Savoy at Reading (1936). Like Robert Cromie, he also drifted into
office developments in the fifties, and he died in 1960, failing to earn an
obituary in any of the usual technical journals.

William R. Glen was another very active and prolific architect for the
Associated British Cinemas circuit, of which John Maxwell was Chairman
and Managing Director. His output was mainly in the midlands and
north, and although his planning was distinctive and use of double
staircases effective, the total effect of his buildings was frequently rather
mundane. A superior offering was the Regal, Chesterfield, which he
designed in 1936 in association with the Norwich architect J. Owen Bond.
It was a large cinema for a town of the size of Chesterfield, seating 1907,
and being provided with a Compton organ. It opened on 12 October 1936
and the fulsome publicity in the opening programme was absolutely

The Regal, Streatham (1937).
A typical design by William R.
Glen

The Forum (ABC) in Liverpool
(1931). A. Ernest Shennan's
finest cinema, internally an art
deco masterpiece

The remarkable relief panels on the auditorium walls of the Forum depict New York skyscrapers such as the Chrysler building set in a mythical landscape

typical of hundreds of cinemas in the thirties:

Every day brings fresh development in the Cinematograph Industry, and the Directors, with their fingers on the pulse of the amusement world, have equipped the Regal so that not only is it the most up-to-date theatre of today, but in the march of progress it will continue to keep its place in the forefront of modern theatres. To fulfil this gigantic undertaking neither time nor money has been spared in securing the most scientific knowledge and finest engineering skill.

All this expertise has not been able to ensure that the Regal has emerged unscathed from the seventies. In 1971 the stalls area was converted into a public house, and a new mini-cinema seating 500 created in the old circle area. Glen also designed the elegant and well-sited all-brick Regal in Staines, the Savoy (ABC) in Croydon (1936), the Savoy (ABC), Portsmouth, which opened on 17 July 1937, and the Regals (ABC), in Streatham (1937), Stoke Newington and Holloway Road, London.

W. T. Benslyn was a later partner of Robert Atkinson and produced many excellent cinemas including the Gaumonts at Smethwick (1930, bingo), Taunton and the Gaumont Palace, Birmingham (1931). A. Ernest

Hurley Robinson's immaculate drawings for the Beaufort cinema, Meriden, a superb cinema in the Jacobean style, only pulled down in 1979

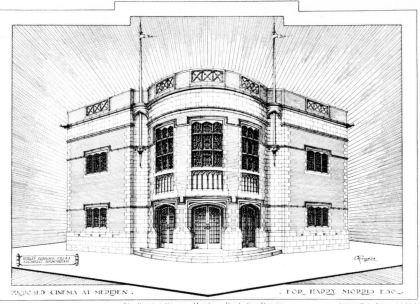

The Beaufort Cinema, Meriden. Perspective Drawing

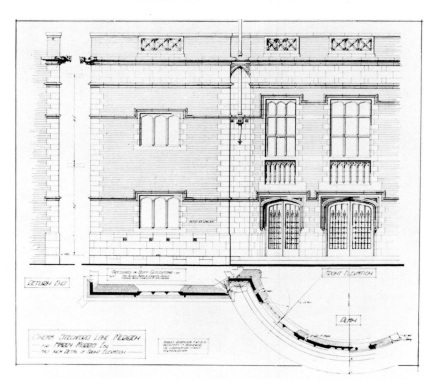

Shennan was a successful Liverpool architect who became Lord Mayor of the City. He designed several of the best cinemas in the city including the Plaza (1928) in Allerton Road; the Mayfair; the Forum (1931); the Abbey, Wavertree (later a Cinerama theatre that closed in 1979); and the Curzon (1936). The Forum (ABC), which opened on 16 May 1931, was designed in association with William R. Glen, and seats 1500. Right in the city centre on Lime Street, its beautiful art deco interior earned the praise of the eminent Professor Reilly. Still intact, although threatened with bingo, it is a cinema well worth preservation and was statutorily protected in 1981.

Hurley Robinson was a Birmingham architect, born in 1884, who designed more than 50 cinemas all over the country, although his main buildings were concentrated in and around his home city. Three of his best known cinemas were the Bristol in Bristol Street, the Ritz, Bordesley Green and the Grand in Soho Road, all completed in the late twenties. The Rialto, Hall Green had an auditorium, which was in the words of the architect, 'conceived in classic vein . . . In the Warrior's Ring, encircling the dome above the balcony, the Imperial spirit is reflected in a number of decorative trophies and martial emblems which adorn the walls and balcony front. The arch, which spans the ceiling, forms a canvas for vigorous oil paintings, depicting an epic struggle between Olympic teams, in which rival charioteers urge their steeds to triumph'. It all sounded a bit overheated for a Birmingham suburb. The Beaufort, Meriden survived intact until its demolition at the beginning of 1979, to be replaced by an example of a new British institution called the 'Texas Homecare' store. It was an extraordinary and unexplained 'Jacobethan' exercise, both inside and out. The brick and 'Guildstone' exterior, was much in the manner of a Jacobean manor house, with mullioned and transomed windows and stained glass leaded panes. Inside the foyer was similarly Jacobean with carved oak panelling and an impressive oak staircase, with carved newels and oriel windows leading to the circle lobby. The 1850 seat auditorium had half-timbered walls and ceiling in the style of a Tudor great hall. Hurley Robinson was a prolific, if relatively little-known, cinema designer throughout the thirties, but apart from the Beaufort, he cannot be said to have produced any really distinctive or outstanding cinema. He died in 1953.

J. Stanley Beard was responsible for a number of notable cinemas around London. Partner in a busy general practice, his first cinema to attract notice was the Capitol, in London Road, Forest Hill (1928), a cinema of fairly small dimensions, but surprisingly successful in its planning in view of the very cramped and steeply sloping site. The interior decoration is not distinguished, but the hybrid style front remains a vigorous and colourful exercise in faience tiling. After closure in 1974, demolition seemed certain, but with the collapse of the property boom, the cinema re-opened as a bingo club in 1978. The most important of Stanley Beard's London projects was a group of six cinema theatres for an entrepeneur named Herbert A. Yapp. Three of these were the well-known Forum cinemas in Fulham Road, Ealing and Kentish Town. The last two are virtually identical, one survives tripled as the Ealing ABC, while the other (which opened on 17 December 1934) remains as a ballroom. The front façades have the same quasi-Egyptian detailing of black columns set against white faience, with unadventurous but elegant domed classical interiors each seating over 2000. Best of the trio is the altogether superior Forum (now the ABC) in Fulham Road, which was the first to open on 18 December 1930. Occupying a prominent corner site, the fine auditorium has been ruined in recent years by subdivision into four. Formerly it was roofed in red fabric like a vast silken tent, and there was elegant classical detailing around the walls. Beard's last prominent

The Forum, Kentish Town (1934), last of J. Stanley Beard's Forum group designed for Herbert Yapp

The beautiful auditorium of the Forum (ABC) in London's Fulham Road by J. Stanley Beard. Its tented fabric ceiling has been destroyed by subdivision

London cinema was the first to go, the small 489 seat Classic, Baker Street, which opened on 23 October 1937 and was demolished in 1973 to make way for the predictably neo-Georgian completion of the terrace in which it stood.

In the thirties, David Evelyn Nye designed a number of cinemas for Shipman and King, including the Embassy cinemas at Esher, Peterborough (1937) and Petts Wood near Orpington, (opened in 1936 and demolished in 1978), and the elegant Astoria at Ashford, Middlesex, now used for bingo. All were notable for their architectural good manners, and the care with which they were fitted into their surroundings. Leslie Kemp and Tasker were another distinguished practice and reference has already

Detail of the bold and elegant designs in the auditorium of the Forum in Fulham Road

Studios 1 and 2 in Oxford Street, London, designed by Kemp and Tasker in 1936

The Havana, Romford, an Odeon imitation – and now the Odeon – designed by Kemp and Tasker in 1936

been made in chapter 3 to Kemp's work in the twenties. Their best-known cinema was opened in 1936, the Studios 1 and 2 in Oxford Street, London, famous for its vivid vertical neon illuminations at night, neon being another notable thirties innovation. What made Studios 1 and 2 unique was that they were the first example of two small cinemas built one above the other, and also incorporating offices and a flat for the owner, Sir David J. James. In 1933 they designed the Commodore cinema in Sevenoaks Road, Orpington, and in 1936 the Mayfair in Whitechapel and the Havana at Romford (now the Odeon), both typical large outer suburban cinemas. Another fine cinema designed by Leslie Kemp during this period was the Ritz, Hereford.

Blackmore and Sykes were a prominent Hull practice, who designed the important Carlton cinema in the mid-twenties, already referred to in

Green's Playhouse, Dundee (1936). One of Alexander's grandest interior schemes for a famous cinema. Note the 'U' in Playhouse deliberately mounted crookedly to denote an advertising gimmick 'U need us, we need U'

chapter 3. In 1936 they designed the luxurious Dorchester cinema in the city centre. Drury and Gomersall were a Manchester firm, perhaps best known for the partner Drury who produced a celebrated series of text-books on construction in collaboration with Jaggard, essential reading and a source of plagiarism for every student of architecture after the war. Joseph Gomersall designed the cinemas, and they were highly regarded in the thirties for their excellent construction and design. More recently they have not fared well and a number have been demolished including the Regent, Fallowfield, Manchester (1929), and the Regal, Altrincham (1931). In 1936 Drury and Gomersall designed the Verona Cinema at Guide Bridge, Ashton-under-Lyne, which became an Odeon even before opening! In 1937 they designed an original Odeon, that at Warrington, which is still open.

The Newcastle firm of M. Alexander and Sons were well known in the north-east throughout the twenties and thirties. Like Komisarjevsky, their director John Alexander specialised in the decorative schemes for

One of John Alexander's
unique and beautiful
perspective drawings of
cinemas he designed in and
around Newcastle

cinema interiors, usually leaving the construction of the building shell to
architects, surveyors or engineers. In the twenties he designed many
complete smaller cinemas and during the late twenties and early thirties
his work anticipated the art deco motifs that were later to become the
trademark of the Odeon style. He was responsible for the manufacturing
process as well as design, and produced much fibrous plasterwork,
mythical composition figures, and elaborate timber templates for decorative painted effects. Although he worked mainly in and around Newcastle, and the smaller towns of Durham and Northumberland, John
Alexander designed interiors elsewhere, notably Green's Playhouses in
Glasgow and Dundee; the Northwick, Worcester (1938); and the Essoldo,
Brighton.

A startlingly art deco interior by John Alexander: the Northwick cinema in Worcester (1938), still intact and used for bingo

What distinguishes Alexander's output is the remarkable record he left of his work until retirement in 1954 in the form of a series of coloured perspective drawings of each scheme, prepared chiefly for his own pleasure and satisfaction. They indicate the exquisite pastel elegance of his super cinema interiors in Newcastle as well as Stockton-on-Tees, Gateshead and Wigan, all now lost or repainted. The solitary scheme to survive intact is the art deco work at the relatively small 1000 seat Northwick, Worcester, now a bingo club and painted in the wrong colours, but preserving the superb mythical figures, horses and chariots flanking the proscenium arch, designed and manufactured in 1938 at a cost of £1138.

Before concluding, a few words should be included on some individual cinemas elsewhere. Cinemas were built prolifically in Scotland, Dundee, for example, having as many as 28 in the thirties, serving a population of under 200,000. Some excellent cinemas were built, notably the very fine Odeon in Edinburgh (formerly the New Victoria), the George in Portobello near Edinburgh (1938), the Cosmo in Glasgow (1939), and, perhaps finest of all, Green's Playhouse in Dundee, designed by John Fairweather, the Glasgow architect, for George Green Ltd, a family firm from Preston, Lancashire that had begun life as travelling fairground showmen. Fred Green, who ran the firm in the thirties, had visions of a chain of super cinemas in the north of England and Scotland to rival anything in America, and although his vast cinema in Glasgow had opened a decade earlier, Dundee was intended to inaugurate this new circuit of dream palaces. In the event, the Second World War prevented his dream being fulfilled, but Dundee opened on 4 March 1936, and the great foyers, café and ballroom all set a standard of luxury never again equalled in Scotland. Another splendid Scottish cinema by John Fairweather is the Playhouse, Edinburgh, which opened on 12 August 1929 and seated 3048. After closure in 1973 the decision was recently taken to restore the superb auditorium to live theatre use.

One of the finest, least altered and latest in date of the super cinemas was designed in the somewhat unlikely setting of the quiet south Essex suburb of Grays. It was called the State and it opened on 5 September 1938, being designed by F. G. M. Chancellor of the famous theatre practice of Frank Matcham and Company for Frederick's Electric Theatres. It remains an independent cinema to this day, still open but threatened with closure; a fairly conventional 2100 seat auditorium with an excellent three-manual Compton organ, and a spectacular brick exterior with a monumental tower dominating the whole composition. The opening night programme was unusually effusive, even for these adulatory times: 'Behind every great enterprise there is always a master mind, a presiding genius to gather the threads of scarcely formed ideas and weave them into facts. Such is Mr A. E. Abrahams – the Man behind the State'. Was that more of a threat than a promise?

Two other cinemas in London deserve notice. First the Warner cinema in Leicester Square, which opened in 1938 and was built on the site of the celebrated old Daly's Theatre. Designed by Edward A. Stone with an interior by Tommy Somerford (the same partnership that created the London Astoria circuit), the exterior is a flamboyant, strongly art deco design. Lastly, the original Curzon in Mayfair, designed by Sir John Burnet, Tait and Lorne, which opened in 1934. It was small (seating only 500), luxurious, and, behind the brick exterior inspired by Willem Marinus Dudok, was a simple and beautifully detailed interior strongly rooted in the Modern Movement. It was plain to the point of starkness, but was a great critical success, and it was also the first purpose-built 'art' cinema in London. It is also a historical fact that although the Curzon was influential, it was not copied. In the event, few architects would have been able to follow the concepts of the Modern Movement even if they had wanted to, when the moguls above all wanted ornate or fantasy

The Warner, Leicester Square, designed in 1938 by Edward A. Stone to occupy the site of Daly's Theatre. Note the strong art deco influence, even at this late date

decoration. Another significant, if relatively minor, off-shoot of the Modern Movement in cinema design was the construction in Britain of several news theatres. The idea of cinemas devoted exclusively to newsreel, cartoon and travel film programmes began in New York in 1929, and was first copied here at the Shaftesbury Avenue Pavilion in 1930. It was not until a Scottish architect, Alister MacDonald, designed news theatres in London at Victoria Station (1933) and Waterloo Station (1934) that they assumed a recognisable identity, for these were adventurous reinforced concrete buildings, and in the case of Waterloo, boldly cantilevered over the station concourse in a curvaceous manner suggestive of Le Corbusier.

Two subsidiary aspects of the super cinemas of the thirties should be noted; one might almost call them subcultures of the genre. These were the cinema cafés and the organs. The café restaurants were as much a part of the planning complex of a large super as the auditorium or the ballroom, and it should be remembered that in their heyday the largest cinemas, with their attendant cafés and ballrooms, were regarded as much as anything as civic amenities, of which the local mayor could

The thirties cinema café par excellence, complete with palm. The Regent, Sheffield, designed by W. E. Trent

declare himself very proud. They were used primarily for luncheons and teas and were always noted for courteous service and reasonable prices. They thus became something of a haven for middle-class ladies meeting for a lengthy chat, and for little boys accompanied by mother meeting elderly aunts over a pot of tea. They were also the haunt of the Palm Court orchestras and trios. In fact they were as much a symbol of the thirties as the Busby Berkeley musicals that were being shown next door on the screens. In the thirties you could eat a passable four course luncheon with roll and butter and coffee for as little as 1/6d. And, incidentally, in the cinema itself you could frequently order tea or coffee to be brought on a tray to your seat in the interval. Perhaps the best-known image of the cinema café was the soda fountain dispensing elaborate confections of the sundae variety. The cinema cafés disappeared much more quickly than the cinemas themselves and they had fallen out of fashion by the late fifties. Today, only two are left in the whole country at the Futurist, Birmingham and the Odeon, Southampton.

Organs, on the other hand, have generated much more enthusiasm in recent years. These electric monsters were originally developed by an Englishman, Hope-Jones, who went to America and basically designed the first Mighty Wurlitzer with electric action and a movable console that would loom up from the Stygian depths below the stage into view of the audience, with organist already in full flow. This mighty monster had an average of four manuals, entailing about 200 stop keys and about 60 pistons involving as much as 100 miles of wiring. Its greatest claim was that it could imitate not only the effect of a full orchestra, but every instrument in it. Any tune could be played, any effect imitated; even drums, cymbals, castanets, sleigh bells and whistles could be operated electrically by remote control. Their consoles were frequently themselves minor masterpieces of art deco design with changing light sequences.

A splendid example of a
cinema organ: the Granada,
Tooting. Now, alas,
unplayable

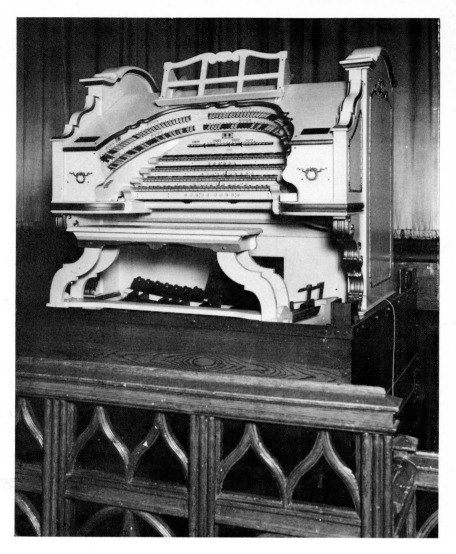

Some well-known names made their reputations at the consoles of the
Comptons or Mighty Wurlitzers in the thirties, principally the three
famous 'Reginalds', Dixon, Foort, and Porter-Brown. Today, few organs
have not been cannibalised in order to obtain parts to repair others, and
even fewer remain in situ and regularly played. Those that do survive are
jealously guarded by their own national preservation society.

Lastly a few words about style, plan and construction. Stylistically
one cannot categorise the super cinemas; in a sense the super cinemas as a
whole created their own style. Many were 'modernistic' in intention, if
not in achievement, but they still remain as the group of buildings in
Britain that best display and typify the outward use of art deco motifs. The
largest group were neo-classically inspired: in effect their decoration had
grown straight out of the British theatres of an earlier era, and also the
American cinemas of Thomas Lamb. John Eberson and his American
atmospherics were widely admired and widely copied, but ultimately
without the elaboration and flair that characterised them in France,

Australia or South Africa. In the initial success of the London Astoria chain, the Finsbury Park Astoria was the nearest Britain approached to a genuine Eberson atmospheric. Even a lavish suburban atmospheric like F. Edward Jones's Regal, West Norwood (now closed), which was built for H. and G. Kinemas and opened in January 1930, had a curiously uncertain 'cardboard' look about it, as though the designer (who was responsible for the original cinema in Madame Tussauds) had not quite made up his mind how far he could go and still stay within the acceptable bounds of good taste. Another disadvantage of the British atmospherics has been their latterday tattiness. Where the 'hard-top' school has relied on 'solid' architectural effects and details that have worn well and lasted, the more insubstantial and fragile foliage, garlands, paintings and lighting effects of the atmospherics have not stood the test of time so well, and have ultimately failed through lack of maintenance.

The planning of super cinemas of the thirties broadly fell into three categories. First, the one floor type, a leftover from the earlier cinema halls, where there are stalls only on a fairly level floor, though sometimes more steeply raked to improve sightlines. Secondly, the stadium type where the front seats conform to the conventional stalls alignment, but behind a cross-aisle, the rear seats are very steeply banked off the stalls floor with stepped aisles, as in a circle. Finally, the most common single balcony type, where a cantilevered circle overhangs a substantial area of the back of a conventional level stalls area, thus increasing seating capacity without impinging on sightlines. The prevailing site conditions tended to dictate whether an auditorium was fan shaped or had to be designed with a straight back and sides in the form of a simple rectangle. The more imposing super cinemas naturally were more often fan shaped.

Constructionally almost all cinemas were designed using the latest available knowledge of modern steelwork, although occasionally reinforced concrete was used in a limited capacity. However it was the versatility of structural steel, that enabled a quick building operation, that virtually eliminated any choice in the matter. Generally, therefore, the steel frame was clad in a brick box, often of cheap flettons, and quite frequently faced on the front in reconstructed stone, or faience tiling. The use of large areas of faience tiling was one of the most distinctive innovations of the cinema building. Usually cream or buff coloured, these velvety-glazed facing blocks first came into fashion early this century and came in a variety of sizes ranging from brick-size to squares as large as 2 ft, and could be moulded or brightly coloured, as desired. The principal manufacturer was Doulton. They became a trademark of thirties commercial building and their great advantage, apart from the individual character that they gave to the cinema, was that they were relatively self-cleansing. Thus they slowed up the process of a building becoming grimy, provided the faience surface had an occasional wash-down. Another material redolent in its associations with the thirties, and often used in conjunction with faience, was Vitrolite, a tough, shiny and durable opaque sheet that formed a good facing for cinema entrances. Roofs were usually tiled or covered in corrugated asbestos. Building a cinema had to be cheap in terms of volume and bulk, and, above all, quick.

With the failure of British cinema architects to establish a consistent pattern of quality in the atmospheric interiors, and the majority opting for

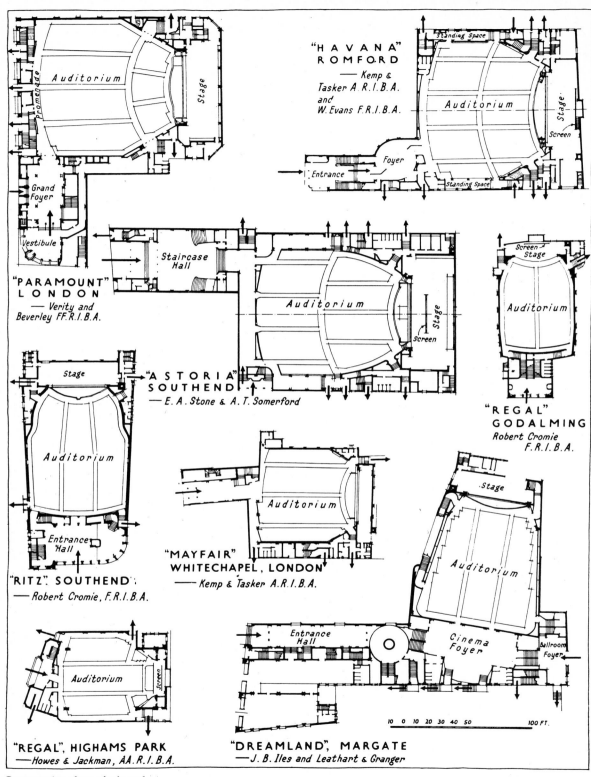

Auditorium

Stage

"HAVANA" ROMFORD
— Kemp &
Tasker A.R.I.B.A.
and
W. Evans F.R.I.B.A.

Standing Space

Auditorium

Stage

Screen

Foyer

Entrance

Standing Space

Promenade

Grand Foyer

Vestibule

"PARAMOUNT" LONDON
— Verity and Beverley FF.R.I.B.A.

Staircase Hall

Auditorium

Stage

Screen

Screen Stage

Auditorium

"REGAL" GODALMING
Robert Cromie F.R.I.B.A.

Stage

Auditorium

Entrance Hall

"RITZ" SOUTHEND
— Robert Cromie, F.R.I.B.A.

"ASTORIA" SOUTHEND
— E.A.Stone & A.T.Somerford

Auditorium

"MAYFAIR" WHITECHAPEL, LONDON
— Kemp & Tasker A.R.I.B.A.

Stage

Auditorium

Entrance Hall

Cinema Foyer

Ballroom Foyer

Auditorium

Screen

"REGAL", HIGHAMS PARK
— Howes & Jackman, AA.R.I.B.A.

"DREAMLAND", MARGATE
— J.B.Iles and Leathart & Granger

10  0  10  20  30  40  50        100 FT.

Comparative plans of selected
thirties cinemas

120

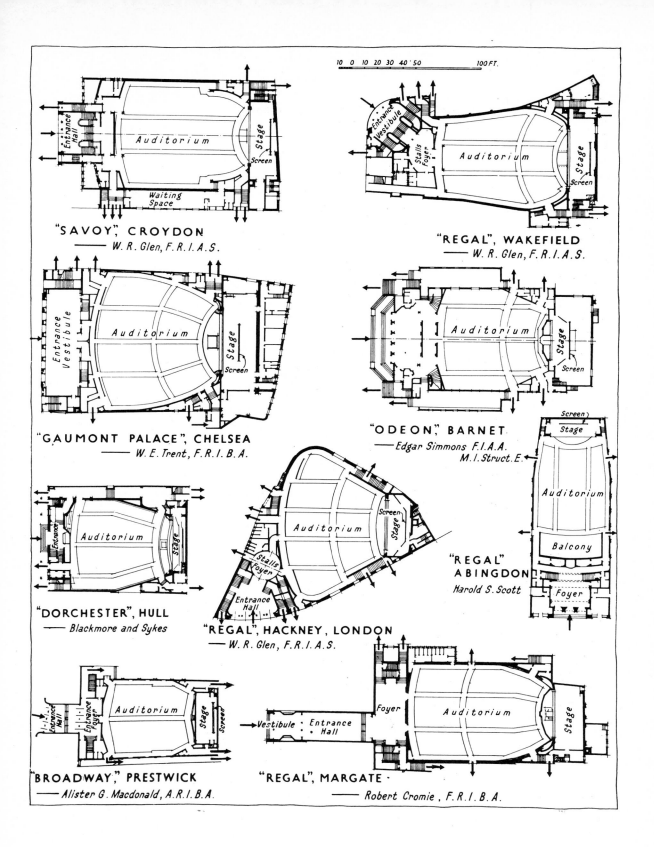

"SAVOY", CROYDON
— W. R. Glen, F.R.I.A.S.

"REGAL", WAKEFIELD
— W. R. Glen, F.R.I.A.S.

"GAUMONT PALACE", CHELSEA
— W. E. Trent, F.R.I.B.A.

"ODEON", BARNET
— Edgar Simmons F.I.A.A.
M.I.Struct.E.

"DORCHESTER", HULL
— Blackmore and Sykes

"REGAL", HACKNEY, LONDON
— W. R. Glen, F.R.I.A.S.

"REGAL" ABINGDON
Harold S. Scott

"BROADWAY," PRESTWICK
— Alister G. Macdonald, A.R.I.B.A.

"REGAL", MARGATE
— Robert Cromie, F.R.I.B.A.

★ **NOTTINGHAM GOES GAY**

# "VITROLITE" at the Savoy Cinema

The Savoy Cinema, Nottingham, is another example of "Vitrolite" doing a bright job. From the ground up to the canopy is black "Vitrolite." Above that is green agate "Vitrolite" with strips of the black. The two side columns and centre feature are in bent green agate "Vitrolite," while black "Vitrolite" has again been used for the centre column.

*Architect:* R. W. Cooper, A.R.I.B.A., Queen's Chambers, King Street, Nottingham. *Fixers:* Messrs. Conway & Co., Manchester.

If you have not got a copy of "Vitrolite" Specifications, which contains technical data and various internal and external "Vitrolite" schemes, write for a copy to the British Vitrolite Co. Ltd., Head Office and Showrooms: 7 Albemarle St., London, W.1. Branch Office: 25 High St., Doncaster.

'Vitrolite' is the registered trade mark of The British Vitrolite Co. Ltd.

the safer option of classically derived interior decorations, the field of imaginative approaches was left more or less to George Coles, who could orchestrate a masterpiece almost at will in any style he chose, and to Theodore Komisarjevsky, who demonstrated in his Granada interiors that there was still one avenue of cinema design, not explored previously, that could be exploited with total success. There was also, of course, the creation of the Odeon style, a cavalcade of cinemas in the first totally recognisable house style that at the same time extended the frontiers of art deco design in building.

The super cinemas designed by the architects described in this chapter remain as the most tangible and characteristic evidence of the remark-

Fibrous plaster mould for the Northwick, Worcester, photographed in John Alexander's workshop in 1938. A pair cost £1138

able and contradictory era that formed the thirties, and the popularity of the film and the cinema is sufficient witness to its importance. In 1939 Kelly's Directory for the old inner London Boroughs that made up the LCC area listed 327 cinemas. Today the number of cinemas that are still open in the same area is less than a hundred: and it is an area that includes the greatest British concentration of cinemas in the West End. That is the measure of the architectural and social importance of the super cinema within the context of its own time, and its subsequent impoverishment. An era, it should not be forgotten, that lasted for only just over a decade from the advent of the talkies in 1928 until the outbreak of war in 1939.

123

# A RUSSIAN DESIGNER OF VENETIAN PALACES

**The perfect dream-child of the thirties**
SIR JOHN SUMMERSON describing the
Granada, Tooting in 1972

THEODORE KOMISARJEVSKY was a man of such varied activities that it is doubtful where his first love resided. The son of Professor Theodore Komisarjevsky, the first tenor of the St Petersburg Opera, and Princess Marie Kourzevich, he was born in Venice in 1882. His early background was as cosmopolitan as his later career, for his childhood was spent in Russia, where he was brought up in St Petersburg, educated at the University and eventually became a student at the Imperial Institute of Architecture, a training that was to become evident both in his stage settings and his designs for cinema interiors. After graduation, he moved to Moscow and diverted his attention to the theatre, first appearing as a producer for the stage in 1907. In 1910 he was appointed producer at the Nezlobin Theatre, and then became manager of his own theatre. He remained there until 1913, and then after the Revolution was invited first to become Director of the Imperial Theatre and then the Moscow State Theatre, a most influential post for a young man in his early thirties. During the next six years he had a significant success in the Moscow theatre with his stage productions whose casts frequently included his

*On previous page* Granada, Tooting: proscenium arch from circle

Theodore Komisarjevsky: a picture taken in the thirties

sister Vera, a leading actress who had created the part of Nina in Tchekhov's *The Seagull* in 1898. He worked also for a time with the Moscow Grand State Theatre of Opera and Ballet. He retained this position until 1919, when he decided to leave Russia for good, and came to settle in England.

He brought an imaginative flair to the London theatre scene that was revelatory in the years following the First World War. Initially his first major success as a producer was at the invitation of Sir Thomas Beecham, with Borodin's *Prince Igor* at Covent Garden in 1919. Another famous exploit in the world of opera was when he mounted Wagner's *Parsifal* with only two days for rehearsal, the result, not surprisingly, being near-chaos. However, as the *Dictionary of National Biography* puts it, he 'had greater influence than any other producer on methods of direction, acting, setting and lighting'. His reputation continued to grow until in 1925 he acquired, under the auspices of Philip Ridgeway, the lease of a small cinema at Barnes on the outskirts of London, and converted it into a theatre, forming his own company. Among those who joined him were Martita Hunt, Edith Evans, Elisabeth Bergner, Charles Laughton and a very young John Gielgud, and this repertory company soon became nationally celebrated.

He rapidly became a luminary also in the London social scene, and his popularity and charm towards the opposite sex was such that faced with his almost unpronounceable name, he soon became affectionately known as 'come and seduce me'. He was not a startling or particularly prepossessing man to look at. Balding, medium in height, he had a pale face enlivened by large brown eyes; his manner to all was restrained and marked by an unexpectedly quiet voice. However, as Sir John Gielgud has remarked, he could on occasion be cruel, aloof and destructive, and above all he never permitted any slipshod or inadequately prepared work. Living up to his popular reputation, he married three times, first Elfrieda di Jarosy, secondly Dame Peggy Ashcroft, whom he married in 1934 and divorced in 1937, and finally Ernestine Stodeile. It was in the late twenties that Komisarjevsky met a rising entrepreneur in the entertainment business, Sidney Bernstein. It was to lead to an association so fruitful as to form the basis of Komisarjevsky's main fame today.

As the new super cinemas became larger and more elaborate, so rivalry between the cinema chains developed, each trying to outdo the other in creating a distinctive house style. It was into this atmosphere in 1930 that Sidney Bernstein decided to launch his Granada circuit, and he chose Theodore Komisarjevsky as his interior designer.

But first Bernstein asked Komisarjevsky in 1930 to work on his new Phoenix Theatre in Charing Cross Road, London. The exterior was designed by Sir Giles Gilbert Scott, assisted on the structure by Bertie Crewe and Cecil Masey, and, to use Bernstein's own description, the interior was conceived 'by emphasising those elements of luxury and comfort peculiar to the architecture of the Italian Renaissance princes'. This was Komisarjevsky's first attempt at designing what amounted to a stage setting within a structural framework. He wrote at the time, 'I was perplexed in the extreme as to how it could be done in a modern structure of iron and cement, in a box-like building with all sorts of erratic unsymmetrical angles, awkward corners, jutting beams and gaping apertures where they were least desirable, in fact with everything which could be guaranteed to scare and annoy old Bramante himself!' However, he soon regained his customary confidence, and liberally helping himself to details from Raphael, Michelangelo and Bramante went on to produce the splendid interior that still survives, with Vladimir Polunin executing the mural panels after originals by Italian masters. Much of this detailing was afterwards to form the model for the pilasters, coffering, grilles and similar enrichments at the Granadas.

Granada, Walthamstow: exterior

So at the age of almost fifty Komisarjevsky had entered a world related, on the one hand, to his first profession of architecture and, on the other, to his adopted home in the live theatre. He was unleashed first upon the unsuspecting cinema-going public in 1930 at the Granada, Dover. Modesty was never his strongest suit, for he was confident enough about his interior here to boast, 'I succeeded in producing an effect of architectural harmony, of richness, and at the same time of restfulness'. The style of decoration adopted was Moorish, and ideas culled from the Alhambra Palace at Granada were freely used. The Granada, Dover was a great success artistically and won Komisarjevsky lavish praise from the cinema industry. His future was assured, and later the same year, with even greater elaboration, he again used the Moorish/Spanish style at the Granada, Walthamstow. This cinema has an unusually lively white-painted stucco exterior in Spanish style by Cecil Masey, and the general manner of the decoration is carried through to the ornately decorated interior, now regrettably divided into three, which is clearly the source of much of Komisarjevsky's inspiration at Tooting the following year. The richly ordered proscenium arch and gilded decorated wall grilles use details from the Palace at Cordoba, overlaid with 17th-

Proscenium arch

Side wall of auditorium

century baroque features. Elsewhere there is much classical detail in the foyers, and the flat barrel-vaulted circle lobby looks forward to Tooting. There is also a fine suite of original furniture, with chairs and tables designed by Komisarjevsky himself.

1931 found Komisarjevsky embarking on what is unquestionably his masterpiece, the Granada, Tooting. By now Bernstein Theatres Ltd had

Detail of decorative grille

trumped their rivals, and their designer was able to elaborate his ideas on the creation of stage designs around the walls of a cinema. His idea was to paraphrase accurately a whole architectural style in one auditorium by means of solid composition. Not for him the impressions created by use of lighting effects. In his designs, he aimed to provide a sense of total involvement on the part of the patrons from the moment they entered the building. By creating these amazing interiors in the densely peopled London suburbs, he provided a predominantly working-class population with a fantasy setting for films far removed from drab everyday life and the dole queue, and this entertainment was obtainable at modest expense. Komisarjevsky wrote:

The picture theatre supplies folk with the flavour of romance for which they crave. The richly decorated theatre, the comfort with which they are surrounded, the efficiency of the service contribute to an atmosphere and a sense of well-being of which the majority have hitherto only imagined. While there they can with reason consider themselves as good as anyone, and are able to enjoy their cigarettes or their little love affairs in comfortable seats and amidst attractive and appealing surroundings.

At Tooting, Komisarjevsky turned with total originality to the Venetian Gothic style for inspiration. It is the world of the Palazzo on the Grand Canal, recreated in the midst of south London. The Doge's Palace is never far away, but to describe the achievement with any degree of adequacy, one must commence outside. The architect for the external structure was Cecil Masey, and as a setting for the riches inside he designed a large Italianate front of white artificial stone rising to a large central tower which, although by no means a great work of architecture, is suitably monumental and forms a worthy approach to the wonders within. Komisarjevsky's interior begins with a gigantic main foyer designed in the manner of a medieval baronial hall with minstrel's gallery, carved panelling and heavily beamed ceiling. It is complete down to the sets of original oak and gilded Gothic side tables and chairs specially designed by him. The rear part becomes the stalls lobby, a marble columned hall in the Italian Renaissance style with mirrors to suggest even greater size. The main stairs lead to the circle lobby, and here we enter the medieval Gothic world: a long cloister lined throughout with

Outer foyer

Inner stalls foyer

cusped arches and mirrors, a journey into infinity, an effect invariably
breathtaking on first entering. And so into the 3500 seat auditorium, and
the glory of Venice. The main roof is part coffered, part sky; the walls are
lined by row upon row of cloistered arches and delicate tracery; the
proscenium arch is a series of cusped Gothic pendants. Mural paintings
by Vladimir Polunin of courtly figures of the 15th century line the arched
recesses; the original chandeliers are in situ; until recently the Mighty
Wurlitzer still rose up from beneath the stage. Everything is deep antique
gold in tone, and has hardly been touched since the day it was opened.
Under the deeply coffered circle survive part of the Gothic traceried
balustrades along the auditorium sides for use of standing patrons. The
walls themselves in this area are incredibly lavishly treated with false
windows and ambitiously moulded columns and pilasters. Finding
sources for this decoration is a fascinating task. Apart from the Doge's
Palace, it is the principal 15th-century Gothic buildings on the Grand
Canal that have been the inspiration: the Ca d'Oro, the Palazzo Cavalli,
the Palazzo Pizini and the Palazzo Foscari; but all the time the influence of

13th-century and 14th-century French Gothic is present.

However, after sudden and unexpected closure as a cinema at the end of 1973, its present use as a bingo hall can only be a cause for deep regret, even though one recognises the changing social patterns that have resulted in ever-diminishing cinema audiences and that this is one of the largest cinemas in Britain. The owners first flirted with redevelopment of the site with an office block, and there followed a prolonged period of semi-neglect while the future of this amazing building was negotiated by the various authorities concerned. Eventually, Granada realised the potential of an exercise to carry out the minimum necessary work to convert the building to a bingo club while maintaining the building in its full original glory. So far, the end product has triumphantly justified the means, even if the use is sadly inappropriate to its dignity, and the only major loss has been the loss of the Wurlitzer, which now lies entombed and unplayable beneath the bingo callers' feet.

After the success of Tooting, Komisarjevsky's continued activity in

the field of cinema design was certain, and his work seemed to know no limits, for in 1932 he became a British subject and began an important series of stage productions in Stratford upon Avon, as the first guest producer at the new Memorial Theatre. It was in 1932 that he commenced a celebrated series of Shakespeare productions for the Stratford Festival, although his often startling and unorthodox treatment of the Bard's work earned him much outraged criticism and accusations of having no understanding. *Twelfth Night* and *As You Like It* were followed in 1936 by his greatest critical success, *King Lear*, a production hailed as a masterpiece, where all directorial excesses and superfluous staging were stripped away. Equally lavish praise was heaped upon his *Comedy of Errors* in 1938, greeted as the most popular production of the season. It was a freely modernised version with such bizarre touches as the main male characters sporting pink bowler hats.

At the same time he was staging operas and plays of many other kinds, and inevitably his productions of Russian plays, notably Tchekhov and Gogol, were especially renowned. *The Three Sisters* and *The Government Inspector* respectively represented his finest work, and he also wrote and produced a remarkable dramatic adaptation of Dostoevsky's *Brothers Karamazov*, entitled *The Brass Paperweight*. Throughout this period, he professed to disapprove of the narrow commercial outlook of Shaftesbury Avenue and Broadway and tended to avoid providing obvious vehicles for stars. Even so, he was most successful in these very areas of the live theatre. His work was widely seen in Europe, and he made many trips to America to produce plays on Broadway. In addition to all this, he also somehow found time to teach acting and to write several books on costume and theatre, of which *Myself and the Theatre*, *The Costume of the Theatre* and *The Theatre and a Changing Civilization* were the best known.

To return to his cinema designs, in 1932, Cecil Masey, otherwise exclusively at this time, a Granada architect, designed independently two cinemas, the Pavilion, Kensal Rise and 'Spanish City', later the Odeon, at Northfields near Ealing, and, although unproven by any written record, the originality and brilliance of the relatively small but elaborately decorated Moorish interior strongly suggests Komisarjevsky had a hand in it.

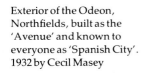

Exterior of the Odeon, Northfields, built as the 'Avenue' and known to everyone as 'Spanish City'. 1932 by Cecil Masey

The auditorium of 'Spanish
City'. It is almost certain that
Theodore Komisarjevsky
designed the interior
decoration

The most tangible evidence is that among the Komisarjevsky drawings of his cinema designs is one of the Northfields cinema. It was
originally called the Avenue Theatre, a dual purpose building in
Northfields Avenue, immediately adjacent to the Piccadilly Line under-
ground station, but soon became generally known as 'Spanish City' to all
the locals, because of its decoration both inside and out. Behind the
colourful white stucco and blue-tiled exterior, an unusually spacious
foyer leads to the auditorium, where the ceiling is formed of billowing
crimson fabric, like a vast tent. Flanking a boldly moulded proscenium
arch are an engaging collection of roofs, balconies, turrets, windows and
grilles, an affectionate parody in miniature of the Moorish village style.
Significantly, the design of the wall grilles is almost identical to what
Komisarjevsky used elsewhere in his Granada schemes, especially
Walthamstow. The Northfields Odeon is threatened with closure following the rejection of destructive plans for sub-division.

In 1933, again with Cecil Masey, Komisarjevsky produced for Sidney
Bernstein the interior scheme for reconstruction of the old Empire
Theatre, Edmonton, which had originally been built to Masey's designs
in 1908. This was a building that was destroyed in the post-war decimation of suburban London theatres. He advised on interiors generally on
the whole Granada circuit during its creation in the thirties but it was in

Side hall of auditorium. One might describe this as semi-atmospheric

Detailing of doors and grilles

Typical suburban brick
Granada at
Kingston-upon-Thames.
Behind the bland exterior lies a
quite elaborate Italian
Renaissance interior by
Komisarjevsky

Granada, Clapham Junction
(1937). After Tooting and
Woolwich, the best
Komisarjevsky interior within
a Masey shell

Exterior of the Granada, Woolwich (1937) by Cecil Masey and Reginald Uren. Strong hints of Dudok brick town halls of the thirties

1937 that he most spectacularly burst back with three more superb interiors. One of these is now lost; the Granada, North Cheam, in an ornate Renaissance style, which was closed in 1969 and subsequently demolished. The second was the Granada, Clapham Junction, tripled in 1973, then turned to Bingo, originally vast in size, again richly Renaissance in decoration behind a rather bland brick exterior by Masey. The story is told here of how with a few days only before opening, the entire auditorium was painted again when the colour was not the precise shade wanted by Komisarjevsky and Bernstein. But undoubtedly the crowning achievement of 1937 was the Granada, Woolwich. Here Komisarjevsky returned to Venetian Gothic for his interior, and there is a conscious effort to repeat the alchemy of Tooting.

The brick exterior by Masey and Reginald Uren is International Modern in concept, with hints of town hall Dudok, and is altogether an outstandingly successful design of its period with its slim advertising tower. Uren designed the famous Hornsey Town Hall the same year in partnership with Slater. The contrast with the interior is such a break that it may have inhibited Komisarjevsky, whose main entrance foyer is rather indeterminate, with an alarming mixture of modern and Renaissance motifs. It wants to be a baronial Great Hall, but it does not quite succeed.

The stunning Komisarjevsky interior of the Granada, Woolwich. Not quite the equal of Tooting, but the detail is fascinating

A fine double-flight staircase with a delicate wrought-iron balustrade has Gothic arches on the landing wall and leads to the circle lobby which, as at Tooting, is in the style of a long cloister, though here suggesting the Moorish style rather than Gothic. It is also wider with an aisle, but its flat pitched ceiling, and mirrors to one side only rob it of the reflective impact of Tooting. Here again, as at Tooting, original Gothic bench seats designed by Komisarjevsky are preserved. Into the Venetian Gothic auditorium, and the space is closely modelled on Tooting. Slightly smaller, overall, the detail has become somewhat coarsened, perhaps through a need for more economy in 1937 than 1931, but it is undeniably still most impressive. The ceiling is not coffered, being divided by beams, and the side walls are dominated by great doorways reminiscent of the Porta della Carta at the Doge's Palace in the way they are handled, though there are stronger echoes of the 13th and 14th-century Gothic style, and motifs from the great portals of the cathedrals at Amiens, Bourges, Rouen and Lyons can all be identified. Lyons is the closest source but Komisarjevsky, with cavalier disregard for niceties of style, inserts a rounded Romanesque arch under the pointed canopy. The proscenium is narrower and more vertical in proportion, but the cusped pendants are similar to Tooting. The cinema closed in 1966 and the interior has suffered since through bingo use.

By now, the Granada circuit was almost complete and Komisarjevsky's work was done. From 1934 onwards, he spent much of his time in the United States where he finally settled at the outbreak of war, and he remained there semi-retired until his death at the age of 71 in April 1954, at Darien, Connecticut. Nevertheless, he retained his British nationality and always planned to return to settle again in London.

How then do we evaluate Komisarjevsky's contribution to cinema architecture? Above all, he was a brilliant man of the theatre, and with him passed England's greatest designer of cinema interiors, who was a scholar in his approach to decoration. Although trained as an architect, he did not (unlike George Coles) design the structures or external elevations that clothed his creations, and it may be fairly remarked that these seldom matched his interiors for either invention or quality. The Granada cinemas were acknowledged as outstanding among super cinemas in the 1930s and he was the only man in Britain to attempt to turn into a semblance of solid architecture the fantasy worlds and lighting effects of the American atmospherics. He was certainly the only man of his era to rival in ability John Eberson and his earlier Palaces of Light. Not only is the Granada, Tooting the most lavishly decorated of all British super cinemas, it can hold its own against the finest anywhere, whether in America, Europe or Australia, and many would claim that it beats them all with ease.

It is all the more curious, therefore, that in spite of his great achievements in cinema design, and obvious confidence in his abilities, he yet remained strangely hostile to the concept of the cinema as opposed to the theatre. He once wrote, 'the cinema does not only cater for imbeciles, it breeds them. The commercial cinema is an entertainment for illiterate slaves'. There seems every chance that his principal buildings will continue to survive as a fitting memorial to a remarkable and versatile man, and a demonstration that the benefits of the theatrical effect can be successfully translated and applied to a cinema interior. No more fitting epitaph can be provided to conclude this chapter than that written at the time of his death by Sir John Gielgud: 'He was a great "metteur en scène", an inspiring teacher, and a master of theatrical orchestration . . . his taste was catholic, his range wide, and his skill in every department of the theatre prodigious'.

# 7

# 'OSCAR DEUTSCH ENTERTAINS OUR NATION'

Always and ever offer entertainment to the public, to allow those who come within its walls to live for an hour or two in the land of make-believe and romance. This purpose should be the controlling influence in its architectural design.

RANDOLPH SEXTON, on cinema design, 1927

I N SPITE OF ITS GREEK ORIGINS – the Odeion of Pericles built on the slopes of the Acropolis – the name Odeon came to mean 'Oscar Deutsch Entertains Our Nation' in the thirties, and it was no idle claim. The whole story of how Oscar Deutsch created the Odeon circuit of cinemas forms probably the most fascinating chronicle of any that illustrate our own British brand of movie madness. Deutsch was the closest British equivalent to the American moguls of the twenties, and it was only the outbreak of the Second World War and his untimely early death in 1941 that prevented his influence being even more widespread.

Oscar Deutsch, son of Jewish immigrants from central Europe, was born in Birmingham in 1893. His father had become rich in the scrap metal trade'and in partnership had founded his own firm of Deutsch and Brenner. His son joined the family firm after leaving King Edward Grammar School, but evidently had already developed his passion for the cinema. In 1920 he left his father's business and went into partnership with two former classmates at school: Michael Balcon and Victor Saville. The company they formed was named Victory Motion Pictures Ltd, with young Oscar Deutsch as its chairman. When Balcon and Saville went into film production in 1923 to make *Woman to Woman*, it was Deutsch who provided most of the financial backing.

Deutsch prospered rapidly and soon acquired the Midlands Amuse-

*On previous page* The bold architectural statement of the unspoiled Weston-super-Mare Odeon, designed by T. Cecil Howitt and opened in May 1935

Oscar Deutsch. A photograph from the 1930s

The first Odeon. The Moorish style Odeon at Perry Barr, Birmingham, opened in 1930, designed by Stanley A. Griffiths and Horace G. Bradley

ment Company, and through that deal control of the Globe and Crown Cinemas in Coventry. Thus, in one easy takeover move, he was into the exhibitor's side of the film business in 1925. He soon ran other cinemas, the Scala, Wolverhampton and the Regent, Tipton, and built his first picture palace at Brierley Hill, Staffordshire, which he rather unimaginatively named the Picture House, and opened on 1 October 1928. In 1930 Deutsch embarked on his most ambitious undertaking to date: it was to build a cinema in the Birmingham suburb of Perry Barr. It was designed by Stanley A. Griffiths and Horace G. Bradley, with a seating capacity of 1638. More significantly, it was where the Odeon name was born, being the idea of Mel Mindlesohn, one of Deutsch's business partners who had just returned from a trip to Greece. Although it bore the name Odeon, Perry Barr had in fact nothing to do with the formation of the Odeon circuit, or the development of the 'Odeon style'. Having opened on 4 August 1930, this rather Moorish domed building was officially taken into the Odeon circuit in August 1935. It closed as a cinema in 1969, and became a bingo club, when the façade was completely reconstructed.

In 1931 Deutsch built another cinema, the 1500 seat Royal at Alfreton, Derbyshire, which was designed by Harry Clayton. By now he was becoming renowned in the trade and he led the successful battle to obtain consent for Birmingham's cinemas to open on Sundays. Then in 1933 he began seriously to build up a chain of cinemas, concentrating at first on the outer London suburbs and the south coast. Five cinemas opened in that year: the Odeons at Weymouth (a conversion of a former bus garage and designed by Harry Clayton), Kingston-on-Thames (designed by Adamson, Marshall and Tweedy on a very narrow site; still used as a bingo club), Canterbury (named the Friars cinema until 1955, designed by Alfred and Vincent Burr), South Harrow (designed by A. Percival Starkey; closed 1972), and Lancing (closed in 1952 and subsequently reconstructed as a factory).

An early Odeon at Surbiton, Surrey. Opened in 1934 to the designs of Joseph Hill, it closed in 1975, and is now a shop

In 1934 Deutsch opened 17 more cinemas, and by now he was by far the fastest growing cinema operator. A. P. Starkey became established as the first of Deutsch's regular architect collaborators, and it is to him that we must credit the use of large areas of cream faience tiling and the idea itself of the creation of an Odeon house style. It was also significant that in 1934 Deutsch started using architectural practices with some of the highest reputations at that time for his cinema designs: Yates, Cook and Darbyshire designed Odeons at Worcester Park (now a supermarket), Tolworth (now a bowling rink) and Wallington (also now a supermarket). Whinney, Son and Austen Hall designed those at Worthing (tripled) and Bognor Regis (now a bingo club); T. P. Bennett and Sons designed the Odeon, Haverstock Hill (closed 1972). This last example is particularly interesting as this was an existing scheme taken over by Deutsch, and it entailed an unusually expensive gold-coloured interior complete with organ. Deutsch generally disliked the extra expense involved in installing electric organs such as Comptons or Wurlitzers, and seldom agreed to their inclusion. However, the one at Haverstock Hill was retained and the superb auditorium with its fan shape and sweeping plaster troughs of concealed lighting in the ceiling was a great success. It was to be Deutsch's London flagship until the Odeon, Leicester Square was completed three years later. George Coles and Andrew Mather, whose practices were to be later responsible for so many of the Odeons in the south-east, also made their debut with Deutsch in 1934: Coles with the Odeon at Welling, Kent (now a bingo club), and Mather with those at Lewes (demolished) and Brighton, Kemptown (now a bingo club). But undoubtedly the most important development of this key year in Deutsch's career was the opening on 22 December of the Warley cinema in Warley (demolished in 1973), for T. Cecil Howitt designed the exterior and Harry W. Weedon, J. Cecil Clavering and Roland Satchwell the interior. It was at this cinema that the great friendship and professional collaboration between Deutsch and Weedon was first formed.

It was in 1935 that the real trademark of the Odeon style first appeared in the Birmingham suburb of Kingstanding: the slim faience-faced advertising tower contrasted with the sleek lines of the more horizontally emphasised brick and faience body of the cinema. Deutsch wanted a recognisable house style above all else, since he was by now fully embroiled in a nationwide competition with other cinema operators at the height of the cinema-building boom in Britain.

It was a fight between the principal film exhibitors, Gaumont-British, ABC, Regal and Paramount that Deutsch joined, and Deutsch also knew that it was the exhibitor with the largest chain who could negotiate the most favourable terms with the Hollywood producers. They, naturally, preferred to do business with rental only. rather than with corporations such as Gaumont, ABC, or Paramount, who were also competitors in the production field. Deutsch's great film coup was with United Artists, for in the early thirties he signed a contract with them that secured first run rights on all their productions in England.

It is no exaggeration to say that it was a considerable ideological battle between the circuits as they vied with each other in terms of style, size and elaboration of their cinemas. Most entrepreneurs wanted elaborate interiors, and their architects generally displayed a natural urge to produce something entirely modern in equipment, and at the same time elaborate and adventurous, to illustrate the unique new medium of the super cinema. Deutsch wanted neither: he did not believe in spending large sums of money on elaborate interiors, and to a large extent he sought a standardisation of exterior design so as to achieve the desired distinctive and always recognisable house style.

The Odeon, Kingstanding (which, oddly, was originally intended for another circuit and was going to be called the Beacon) was designed by Cecil Clavering, then a young assistant in Harry Weedon's office, and there is no doubt that he created a building of brilliant individuality. Clavering's inspiration was Julian Leathart's 'Dreamland' at Margate, and all the elements that were to make up the Odeon style are present, such as the rounded corners and streamlined faience entrance façade. Kingstanding was a tremendous success, both with the public, but more importantly with Deutsch. Harry Weedon's practice, which had previously specialised in housing and industrial projects, became established as his principal firm of architects. Thirteen new Odeons opened in 1935. Andrew Mather's example at Chingford (demolished 1972) was a remarkable building with astonishing verticality in its design, dominated by a splendid tower; it was the best example, other than the Odeon, Leicester Square, of Mather's rather brash but highly effective approach to Odeon design.

Cecil Clavering did not stay long enough in Weedon's office to design many Odeons and in any case one must not underestimate the contribution of Weedon himself to the design process. Harry Weedon was born in 1888 and became an Associate of the RIBA at the age of 24 in 1912. In the same year he designed his first cinema, the Picturedrome at Perry Barr, which was demolished in 1965. Between 1934, when he joined Deutsch's recently formed Odeon Theatre Group, and the outbreak of war in 1939,

The sensational art deco lines of the Odeon, Chingford, which opened in 1935. Designed by Andrew Mather, it was demolished in 1972

Original drawing for the Odeon, Colwyn Bay by J. Cecil Clavering of Harry Weedon's office. Opened in 1936, interior altered

he designed or was Consultant Architect for over 250 cinemas. Ironically, Deutsch's first Odeon was a mere couple of hundred yards away from Weedon's first cinema of 1912 in Perry Barr.

1936 saw the Odeon circuit very rapidly expanding. Deutsch wanted a cinema in the High Street of every town in the British Isles with a population of 25,000 or over, he wanted them designed quickly and built cheaply, and he wanted them to be as near identical as site limitations and the relevant local authorities would allow. Cecil Clavering, now Weedon's chief assistant, had studied architecture at Newcastle-upon-Tyne under Professor Cordingley, and he wrote to Cordingley to find a replacement when he decided to leave Harry Weedon and go to the Office of Works. By now Cordingley had gone to take up the chair in architecture at Manchester, and by luck the letter arrived the very day Robert A. Bullivant was enquiring at the school for work after he had completed his course of study. Bullivant went to Weedon's office the next day, and two days later began work alongside Clavering in the office of which he is now principal.

Before he left, Clavering created three more, relatively similar Odeons at Colwyn Bay (much altered), Sutton Coldfield (tripled) and Scarborough (a most beautiful cinema, still very little altered). Thirty-four other Odeons opened in 1936, of which Harry Weedon's office contributed eight. That at Chester was an odd one out in that it departed from the usual Odeon style because of its historic surroundings, and was designed more expensively as a monumental brick box, a little reminiscent of the Dudok-inspired town halls of the thirties.

By now Odeons were appearing so fast that the pace was almost becoming too much for Weedon's office, who also had to retain executive contact with other architects designing Odeons like Andrew Mather and George Coles. Robert Bullivant recalls the case of the Odeon, Falmouth where late in 1935, Weedon phoned him just before midnight and asked him if he could keep an appointment at 11.00 am the next day in Falmouth. So Bullivant drove through the night the 400-odd miles and arrived the next morning with five minutes to spare. He was shown a site for a cinema (the former Falmouth brewery), spent the rest of the day making a survey, came back to Birmingham and by the end of the week had produced sketch plans. In less than twelve months the cinema was open to the public. As if this programme had not been enough, Weedon had contacted Bullivant in Falmouth to say 'Have a look at sites in St. Austell, in Camborne, and in Redruth, and on the way back call at Taunton'.

Bullivant also remembers the importance Weedon placed on efficient office organisation. When he joined the office, there was only a staff of about six, but within 18 months this had expanded to 140 in order to cope with the Odeon workload. Weedon broke down this number into teams of six and seven, each with a group leader, and Bullivant, who was the vital link with what Cecil Clavering had started, had the job of co-ordination with all of them. Weedon carried out an exclusive brief for

The Odeon, Muswell Hill, 1936, by George Coles. The interior survives as one of the best art deco cinemas in England. Main foyer

Deutsch, in that he not only designed new cinema buildings, but he also vetted the designs of the other architects such as Mather or Coles, who were employed on Odeon projects. Weedon prepared in this connection a comprehensive design brief in conjunction with the Odeon Theatres Technical Department. Another aid to improved efficiency was the preparation of a chart, which conformed to Home Office and LCC regulations, showing six possible arrangements of auditorium seating. Weedon also gave his assistants specially designed boxwood scales divided to show the standard stair tread and riser dimensions, the 20 inch seat widths, and back-to-back seat spacings.

Back to 1936, and the contributions of Andrew Mather and George Coles. Coles designed five cinemas of which Muswell Hill is by far the most remarkable (seating originally 1872 and costing over £30,000), by reason of its splendid interior. In spite of recent changes, the art deco foyer, circle stairs and auditorium ceiling are still intact and display the highest flair and imagination in their design. Andrew Mather's designs for 1936 numbered ten. The opening publicity by Odeon for the opening of his Faversham cinema on 9 March 1936 is typical and makes entertaining reading: 'Every known means of art, science, and hygiene have been introduced to further the comfort of patrons', they said, and went on, 'the truly delightful effects of the ever changing yet restful and mellow colour-

Auditorium of the Odeon, Muswell Hill. Note the 'cash-register' effect of the auditorium

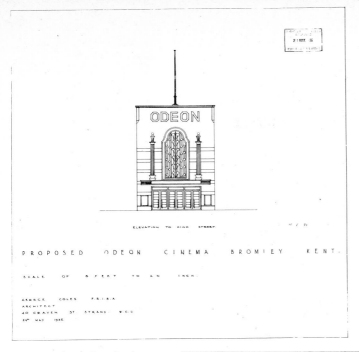

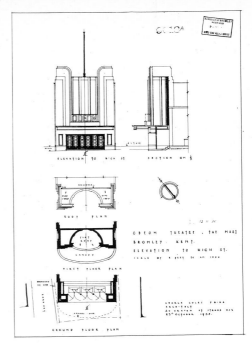

George Coles's plans for the Odeon, Bromley, which opened in September 1936. Note the earlier, safely classical detail of the elevation, and the art deco version which succeeded it.

*Above left* 1st elevation

*Above right* 2nd elevation as built

*Right* Plan

ings, rely mainly upon a wonderful new system of coloured lighting, seen to the best advantage when harmoniously blending on the exquisitely tinted curtain'. A veritable plethora of superlatives, especially since the cinema with its half-timbered auditorium walls is aesthetically wildly inappropriate!

By 1937 Deutsch owned over 300 cinemas, both newly built and purchased from other operators, and now Odeons began to be opened at the rate of as many as two a week. Thirty-six Odeons were built in 1937, including the flagship of the whole operation, the all-black glossy Odeon in London's Leicester Square. Harry Weedon's office contributed 16 of them and Robert Bullivant himself designed four. York is interesting as the only other important example, except for Chester, of an Odeon being adapted to the planning requirements of a historic environment. As at

A typical Andrew Mather
Odeon. Well Hall, Eltham,
London, opened in May 1936

Whinney, Son and Austen
Hall, one of the best
architectural practices of the
thirties, produced this Odeon
at Craven Park, Harlesden,
London, which opened in
1937

Original design by Robert
Bullivant of Harry Weedon's
office for the Odeon, Exeter,
1937

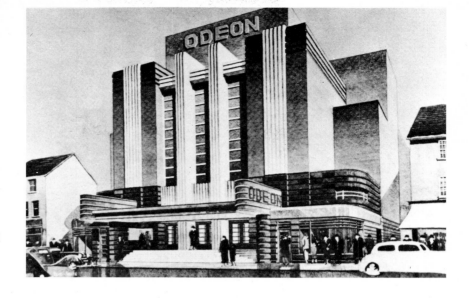

The only Harry Weedon
Odeon of any significance in
London: Swiss Cottage,
opened in September 1937. All
brick, it bears the
unmistakable signs of being a
takeover of a Robert Cromie
scheme

The epitome of the Odeon
style. George Coles's Odeon,
Woolwich, opened in October
1937

Chester, the result is a rather austerely designed and modelled all brick
façade. The Odeon at Swiss Cottage, designed by Basil Herring in
Weedon's office from a scheme taken over from Robert Cromie, is also the
only example, apart from the later Odeon in Hendon, of a London Odeon
designed from Birmingham, rather than by Coles, Mather or one of
several other London-based practices. It is also an uncharacteristic all
brick Odeon of lumpish, flat and square proportions, in fact typical of
Cromie's usual Regal style. The 1937 contribution from George Coles
included Woolwich. It is always a dangerous and inevitably rather subjective judgement to pick a personal favourite, but the Woolwich Odeon
represents externally perhaps best of all, the epitome of that elusively
named 'Odeon style'. Being sideways on to the road, it displays more of
the flowing curves of art deco inspired faience tiling than most, and is
almost reminiscent of the suites of dining room furniture of the period: a
continuous sequence of immaculately detailed curving lines. Designed to
seat 1828 at a cost of nearly £47,000, it survives intact, but with a much
simplified interior.

Andrew Mather's principal contribution in 1937 was in London's
Leicester Square. The Odeon, Leicester Square replaced the celebrated
and exotic Alhambra Theatre where cinematography had begun exactly
40 years before. In the view of many people at the time, the rather flashy
all-black granite cinema with its 90 ft high tower was no substitute for the
well-loved old West End theatre that had occupied the site until the

Sleek lines, art deco motifs and more than a hint of the Egyptian at the Odeon, Woolwich

Original drawing for the all-black Odeon, Leicester Square, 1937. Flagship of the circuit

mid-thirties. Seating 2116, the eventual rather compromise design was by Thomas Braddock, who was then in Mather's office, with Harry Weedon keeping a close executive and consultative contact with developments. Whatever its merits judged on purely architectural grounds, it remains externally a remarkably striking cinema today, and worthy of its place as the centrepiece of Deutsch's Odeon circuit. Unfortunately its interior, with its art deco influences and mythical figures by Raymond Briton Riviere sweeping across the auditorium walls towards the proscenium arch, was savagely and unnecessarily swept away in the name of modernisation in the late sixties, and although there has been a more recent attempt to restore some of the detail (and fortunately the organ), much has been irretrievably lost.

All things considered, 1937 was Deutsch's greatest year for expansion, for he took a controlling interest in the County group of cinemas, and took over two other circuits, London and Southern Super Cinemas, and the Scottish Singleton group. He also arranged for Odeon to become a public company with a share capital of £6 million.

In January 1938 Deutsch announced his plans for overseas expansion to 'two Empire colonies and one foreign country', and it was immediately evident that he had his eye on Canada. Harry Weedon was soon sent to study the state of cinema design in North America. However, the clouds that heralded the Second World War were gathering and long delays began to accumulate in building new Odeons. This in turn led to speculation about the financial stability and viability of the whole Odeon operation.

The superb interior of the
Odeon, Leicester Square
before mutilation in the 1960s

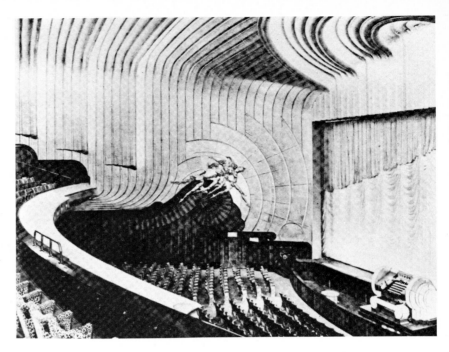

Original drawing for the
Odeon, Leicester, 1938, by
Robert Bullivant of Harry
Weedon's office

Market and trade speculation became rife over the future of Deutsch's
company, as it was plainly apparent that the shortage of steel for construction, and finance generally were severely hampering progress. The
financial problems were remedied by the appearance of a flour magnate
named J. Arthur Rank, who took his place on the Odeon board in January
1939. Nevertheless, to return to 1938, another 25 Odeons were built and
opened, fairly evenly divided between Weedon, Mather and Coles. The
main development in 1938 was the opening of some larger than usual
Odeons in major city centres in direct competition with other picture
corporations, as well as other existing forms of entertainment. Weedon's
office designed examples in Norwich, (demolished), Leicester (tripled,

A natural follow-on from Woolwich. George Coles at the Odeon, Balham Hill, opened in April 1938

designed by Robert Bullivant), and Bradford (demolished, a very large example seating 2713, designed by Bullivant). George Coles designed another fine example in Halifax (now closed), which seated over 2000 and cost almost £60,000. 1938 was Andrew Mather's busiest year for he designed eleven Odeons for Deutsch. They share the usual rather crude and flashy qualities that render his work generally less effective than either Weedon or the endlessly versatile George Coles. Mather tended to use larger faience tile sizes which give his exteriors a rather monotonous and flat appearance, and he often omitted the familiar slim faience-faced advertising tower. His best effort in a clutch of London suburban examples is probably the unusually large Odeon at Peckham, now tripled, which was built on the site of the old Queen's Theatre and cost £43,800 for 2110 seats. His Hackney Road Odeon, which closed in 1961, was the first Odeon to go over to full-time bingo, re-opening as the Top Rank Bingo Club on 21 May 1961.

George Coles contributed six Odeons in 1938, including Balham (recently closed), and Deptford (a fine example, now derelict and under immediate threat of demolition). As with his Odeon at Woolwich, Balham is another of those quite outstanding designs that seem to evoke nostalgically the very essence of the Odeon era, and here also there is a particularly well-preserved interior, complete with its foyer settees and column ashtrays.

Late in 1938 Oscar Deutsch commenced talks aimed at a takeover of the Gaumont-British Picture Corporation. This would have given him control of more than 600 cinemas in Britain and made him the largest cinema circuit. In terms of numbers he was still led by John Maxwell's ABC chain which had been founded early in 1929 and had 474 cinemas in mid-1938. However, like John Maxwell before him, Deutsch failed to buy out Gaumont-British.

1939 still saw the continued development of the Odeon circuit and

157

another seven opened before the declaration of war on 3 September. The outbreak of war naturally put a halt to most of Deutsch's entrepreneurial activities, but one last great coup remained to him: in November 1939 he took over the operation of Paramount's British theatres. This not only brought him the four celebrated London atmospheric Astorias in Brixton, Finsbury Park, Streatham and the Old Kent Road, but also major Paramount cinemas in Manchester, Leeds and Newcastle. Ironically these were the very sort of cinemas he had always resisted building himself; great super cinemas with expensive and lavishly decorated interiors.

The war stopped building operations actually in progress at Worcester, Highgate, and Westbourne Grove, London. Eighteen other schemes on the drawing board or in construction were abandoned completely. The war undoubtedly caught the Harry Weedon organisation by surprise, for 90% of their office staff and resources were being devoted to designing Odeons. But the practice survived the blow and continues to this day as one of the most highly respected architectural offices in the midlands, and after Weedon's retirement, Robert Bullivant assumed senior partnership in the practice as the office widened its workload in the post-war years of rebuilding in Birmingham and they became, among other commissions, architects to Austin Motors. However, Bullivant is found as late as 1956 designing a new Odeon in Sheffield, which is alas already turned over to bingo.

A word should be said here about some other of the cinemas that came over to Odeon, with such events as the County, Singleton and London and Southern takeovers. First, the Singleton takeover, and to a lesser extent the County, gave Deutsch a ready-made circuit of a dozen cinemas in Scotland, and so Odeon film releases were now able to appear in Aberdeen, Airdrie, Coatbridge, Dundee, Falkirk and Glasgow, as well as several smaller towns and suburbs. With an eye to competition close to hand, Deutsch was able to take over no less than five cinemas in Coventry, the Astoria, Globe, Regal, Rialto and Scala, to give him a virtual monopoly in the city centre. The County takeover brought him, for example, the Majestic in Staines, a remarkable but little-known atmospheric that has now been demolished and replaced by a typically indifferent and faceless sixties office block. The County takeover also brought him the Regal in Godalming, Surrey, a neo-Georgian cinema design by Robert Cromie that had won the approval of no less an architect than Sir Edwin Lutyens.

By 1940 Oscar Deutsch had not long to live. Still a relatively young man he had, nevertheless, been enduring a long battle with ill health. Late in 1941 he went into hospital for the latest in a series of stomach operations, and he died on December 5, a victim of cancer at the age of 48. His rise as a cinema owner had been phenomenal. From six cinemas under his control in 1931, he had formed Odeon Theatres Ltd in 1933 and become the eighth largest circuit in Britain. By his death he had built at his expense about 140 cinemas and ran an empire of 278 Odeons, a figure that had exceeded 300 in 1937. It was as one mayor said in 1937, when opening his local Odeon, 'a romance of finance'.

What is the key to the Odeon mystique? The original Odeons (that is the genuine models, not the later takeovers from other circuits) recognisably displayed a house style, and they are now rightly acknowledged as being among the best of any commercial buildings put up between the wars. Occasionally (especially the Andrew Mather examples) they were an undoubted blot on the townscape in their coarse bulk and ill-proportioned detail; more often their clean lines and the simplicity of their faience-tiled surfaces stand them apart as works of real architectural merit, at a time when neo-Georgian was all too often the easy option. Internally the intention was to provide supreme comfort in restful but essentially plain surroundings at a cost of about £20 per seat. They were spacious, usually seating around 1400–1800, but they were not giants like the Paramount Astorias or some of the Granadas. Sightlines were uniformly excellent; decoration, usually endowed with a touch of art deco in the motifs, was mostly confined to the areas flanking the proscenium arch. They were above all a complete break away from both the traditional school inspired in America by Thomas Lamb, and in Britain by Frank Verity, and from the atmospherics that grew out of John Eberson. The Modern Movement theatres and cinemas of Scandinavia and Europe, but more especially Germany, were the source of influence. In particular the work of the architects Fredrich Lipp and Fritz Wilms was evidently known and appreciated, but it is three specific buildings in Berlin whose influence is most clearly marked in identifying the Odeon style: the exterior of the Titania-Palast by Schoffler, Schlönbach and Jacobi, complete with slim advertising tower; the Universum Cinema or Luxor Palast designed by Erich Mendelsohn in 1926–9; and Hans Poelzig's Grosse Schauspielhaus of 1919. There was also the more home-grown influence of Leathart's Margate 'Dreamland' and the work of Joseph Emberton.

The art deco influence is always clearly visible, nowhere more so, when they still survive, than in the light fittings, foyer sofas and column ashtrays. It is as if the Paris Exhibition of 1925 was coming to life again a decade later. An often quoted humourous remark about Odeon interiors is that they were 'Gilded by the Lily', a reference to Oscar's wife, Mrs Lily Deutsch, who brought an entirely welcome atmosphere of art deco influenced taste in the selection of colour schemes. It was her contribution to be consultant for the interior decoration of her husband's Odeons, and the pastel coloured results were always impeccably judged and chosen, all the more so now that these schemes on paper have to be judged against the results of insensitive and self-indulgent colour schemes of the last decade in dark purples, pinks and blues. No more appropriate conclusion can perhaps be drawn to the Odeon story than to quote Oscar Deutsch himself, writing in the journal *Design and Construction* in March 1937: 'It was always my ambition to have buildings which were individual and striking, but which were always objects of architectural beauty . . . we endeavour to make our buildings express the fact that they are specially erected as the homes of the latest, most progressive entertainment in the world today'. He succeeded.

# 8

# THE DECLINE OF THE CINEMA AND ITS SOCIAL FUNCTION

**Prepare Practical Plans for Pretty Playhouses—
Please Patrons – Pay Profits.**

Office slogan of JOHN EBERSON

ORLDWIDE HOSTILITIES were declared for a second time on 3 September 1939, and at first all cinemas were closed down as a safety precaution. However, they were soon allowed to reopen, and when they did they had bigger audiences than ever before. This was more than simple mass escapism, for the cinema newsreels were able to satisfy the thirst for visual news of progress of the war in a manner with which the radio and newspapers were unable to compete. Thus, during the war years, the cinema operators enjoyed what must initially have been an unexpected and unprecedented boom in attendances. It was symptomatic of the 'We never closed' attitudes that prevailed that cinemas very seldom shut down during air raids. The usual practice was for a message to be flashed up on the screen warning of the impending raid and offering patrons the opportunity to leave and collect a refund on the way out. Few people ever took up the offer, and for the majority the film simply continued as usual while the raid happened around them. To some extent, of course, cinemas were much better protection from bombing than most buildings, with their heavy steelwork, non-combustible roof coverings, and even occasionally reinforced concrete roofs. But above all it was the British psyche which triumphed in face of adversity, that spirit that always insists with a stiff upper lip that the show must go on!

The results of the saturation bombing air raids on our cities were horrific in terms of casualties to people, but when all was reckoned up at the end of the war, surprisingly few cinemas had been destroyed beyond repair, although a good many had suffered sufficient damage to close them forever. In spite of the devastation in cities such as London, Manchester, Bristol or Plymouth, relatively few suburban or central cinemas were lost. For example only one Odeon out of 300, the one at Canning Town, east London, was too far damaged to make repair an economic proposition, and this cinema, ironically, had been one of the last to open in 1939, only to survive for two years.

However, as the post-war austerity situation developed, it might have been better in retrospect had there been a few less cinemas around. In the years following the war, cinema attendances began to show signs of falling away dramatically, after an initial surge in the mid-forties, when no doubt the exhausted nation badly needed some diversion and entertainment. There had been approximately 5500 cinemas open at the outbreak of war, and at first the casualties were principally small older cinema halls that were privately owned and forced to close as much by rising overheads and competition from the supers as falling audiences. Even in the fifties the trends were not yet so marked, and the biggest cinema chains tried a little modest expansion after the period of retrenchment during the war years. For example, the Odeon group united with Gaumont-British under J. Arthur Rank's chairmanship, and thus brought together a circuit of over 600 cinemas, comfortably exceeding the previous biggest, John Maxwell's ABC circuit of just under 500 cinemas. Three unfinished Odeon schemes, left over from before the war, were completed. These were at Worcester, opened on 2 January 1950, designed by Robert Bullivant; Westbourne Grove, London, which opened on 29 August 1955, a cost-cutting adaptation by Leonard Allen of the pre-war Andrew Mather scheme; and Highgate, London, which opened on 19 December 1955 and was designed by T. P. Bennett and Son.

*On previous page* The smooth but blandly characterless interior of the Empire, Leicester Square. Larger than most of the recent 'basement' cinemas, it exhibits the same lack of any sense of occasion

Surprisingly, the last was not destined to have a long life, after just 19 years it was closed and demolished to make way for redevelopment in 1974.

Regrettably, cinema design in the fifties was distinguished by its paucity of inspiration and imagination. The post-war shortages and austerity might have resulted in bold simplicity, but instead we were rewarded with pale reflections of the thirties. In this respect the Odeons proved the worst offenders. One of the first was in 1956, the Gaumont (now Odeon) Barnsley by T. P. Bennett and Son. Designed to replace the old Palace Variety Theatre, which was destroyed by fire in 1954, it was completely conventional in concept, seating 1238 in stalls and circle. Much of the plain auditorium was lined with acoustic tiles. It could not be said that the design was in any way offensive, simply that it was rather too obviously a tired re-working of thirties Odeon ideas, overlaid with some Festival of Britain trademarks such as the treatment of railings and lighting fittings. The front façade was pure early fifties in all that represents as a period of uneasy architectural transition, as designers strove to find a new vocabulary after the war, being quite flat and arranged as a series of brick panels, some light, some dark, divided by concrete ribs, with some containing windows. Also in the same year Robert Bullivant designed a new Odeon in Sheffield, but the most interesting cinema building of the fifties was undoubtedly Wells Coates's Telekinema, designed in 1951 for the Festival of Britain. In 1952 it became the first National Film Theatre, run by the British Film Institute, but it was by its very exhibition purpose a temporary building, and it was demolished in 1957 when the NFT moved to its new home under the arches of Waterloo Bridge. Two other prominent fifties cinemas deserve a mention: the Cecil Cinema, Hull, built in 1955 on the site of the old Cecil Theatre, and the preposterously named Drake Cinema, built in Plymouth in 1958 complete with a galleon in full sail planted on the front façade.

In 1959 the Columbia in London's Shaftesbury Avenue was completed to the designs of Sir John Burnet, Tait and Partners, and ushered in a depressing new image for the city centre cinema, consigning it to the bargain basement of a new office development.

The sixties brought a decade of expansion, or more accurately modernisation, as the Rank Organisation built a total of seven new cinemas. None of these were particularly distinguished, unlike the numerous new cinemas being built, for example, in Germany. British designers seemed to have nothing original to contribute. The first was the Odeon in Harlow New Town, designed by W. J. Hughes in 1960, a disappointing exterior, but much more successful inside with a spacious 1250 seat stadium-type plan. The Odeon in London's Haymarket followed in 1962, built on the site of the Capitol cinema, and like the Columbia relegated to the basement of a new office development. In 1963 a new Odeon opened in the Merrion Centre, Leeds and another in Leicester in 1964, reconstructed out of the old Gaumont. In 1966 the new Odeon at Marble Arch, designed by T. P. Bennett and Son, again spectacularly demonstrated how the image of the cinema can disappear almost without trace below a high rise office block, reduced to a low single level stadium plan.

However, 1966 also produced the two best post-war cinemas in

The cinema today. The Columbia in London's Shaftesbury Avenue, relegated to the basement of an office block. 1959, architects Sir John Burnet, Tait and Partners

London, neither of them, it must be said, quite the equal of its predecessor. The first was the Odeon, Elephant and Castle, designed by Ernö Goldfinger on the site of George Coles's celebrated Trocadero cinema which had closed for demolition in October 1963. The new Odeon was an excitingly sculpted concrete box, with a stadium plan inside, seating about 1000. Although now looking a little shabby after 15 years, this remains visually the most adventurous of British post-war cinemas. The other 1966 cinema was the Curzon in Mayfair designed by Sir John Burnet, Tait and Partners to replace their famous earlier 1934 Dudok-influenced model. The earlier cinema had been freestanding on a prime site in the area of London with the highest property values, so such luxury was not likely to be permitted again, and indeed the new Curzon sits under a nine-storey office and flat block. Its stadium-type interior is notably spacious and comfortable, and the decorations are highly individual; a deeply coffered concrete slab for a roof with inset lighting, and interestingly abstract sculptured wall panels in glass-fibre by William Mitchell.

Later in the sixties Rank's opened a new Odeon Filmcentre in Swansea, and more recently others at Norwich (1971) and Brighton (the Kingswest Centre 1973). This effectively brings any new cinema construction of note up to date, and it remains to examine the trends of today that had their roots in the fifties and sixties. On the positive side, there have been the technological innovations such as Cinemascope introduced in 1953, Cinerama (1954) and 70 mm film (1958). Cinemascope had the widest effect, in every sense of the phrase, in that many cinemas had to have their proscenium arches widened to take the new screens with their aspect ratio of 2.55:1. Cinerama was far more exciting, but its space requirements have dictated that very few outlets for the technique have ever opened in Britain. Basically it is a multi-dimensional system requiring a specially designed giant curving screen of at least 75 ft width. Originally three projection booths matching three films on the screen were required, although later improvements brought about a single-lens Cinerama system, which was unveiled at Frank Matcham's London Coliseum theatre in 1963.

Ironically, the greatest technological advance of all, first publicly popularised at the Festival of Britain, has proved the catalyst for the cinema: television. As television gained a place in the home and prices of the sets came down with mass production, so cinema attendances went into rapid decline. Older cinemas began to close in droves; the wartime boom in audiences, sustained into the early fifties, was emphatically over. By the end of the fifties, television had taken over as the mass media entertainment, although there was some relief on the horizon in the form of bingo. In the late fifties, cinemas were closing down everywhere, including some of the best thirties dream palaces, and the two major circuits of Rank and ABC grasped very quickly the possibilities of bingo. The first Rank bingo hall opened in Peckham in early 1961, and a few months later the first Odeon to be converted, in Hackney Road, London, reopened on May 21. And so the die was cast of bingo as a great preserver of cinemas.

It has to be said that as television gained popularity in the fifties and sixties, keeping people at home by their firesides, the cinema operators themselves hardly assisted their cause by their policies. While it is true that they reacted by going into bingo with enthusiasm, since they had a ready-made stock of suitable buildings immediately to hand, and later attempted to win cinema audiences back by 'twinning' and 'tripling' operations, they nevertheless, for at least a decade, sat back and watched the audiences slip away from them. Their failure lay in the lost opportunity of booking policy for films. By introducing block booking of films to whole areas at a time, they simply removed the element of choice from their potential customers with the result, for example, that if the same film was showing that week at every Odeon within reach in a particular district, there was no choice to be made, and you either went to your local or you stayed away. There can be little doubt that the cinema circuit promoters lost an incalculable amount of money by this policy, which has only recently been dissipated. In retrospect what also made this policy so counter-productive was that it could so easily have been alleviated by allowing individual cinema managers, who usually knew their local markets very accurately, some freedom in booking the most appropriate films themselves. As recently as the early 1970s it was remarked to the author by a Rank executive that in relation to their size, their three most profitable west London cinemas were the Northfields Odeon, Richmond Gaumont and (then) Gaumont, Notting Hill Gate, all of whose managers enjoyed a certain measure of autonomy in deciding which films were to be shown.

The other area that hastened the decline of the cinema, and incidentially ensured the audiences did stay away from films block-booked into an area, lies in the nature of the films themselves. Without getting embroiled in a discussion about the role of the film, and the extent to which it should justify a minority appeal, the basic fact remains that the mass popularity of the cinema was founded on it being a family entertainment, and that role, with few exceptions, was what it fulfilled up to and throughout the Second World War. Its accepted image was of the place where you could escape to regularly and cheaply with your family, and once there you could 'dream a little'. Through the fifties and sixties, the character of films gradually assumed a more consciously adult tone, and the proportion of X films, forbidden to minors, correspondingly increased. This not only excluded the traditional family element from cinema-going, for many of the new films were not within what might be termed the preserve of Art Cinema. The so-called (in the trade) 'intelligentsia houses' had always occupied a valued and vital place in most cities, and in London there had been the Curzon, the Classics, the Academy, the Cameo-Polys and the Everyman to satisfy even the most discerning tastes. What the new films of the late fifties and sixties brought was a new popular brand of sex and violence, not usually within the context of a foreign 'art' film, and almost invariably these attracted the rating of a X certificate. It is not too fanciful to suggest that the nature of these catchpenny films themselves helped to dictate the character of cinemas of the fifties and sixties: seedy, deteriorating palaces followed by small, plain, anonymous studios of cut-price construction.

During the sixties more and more cinemas closed or were turned into bingo halls, and then in the late sixties when it seemed that television might be going to kill off the cinema altogether, the big circuits came up with a last ditch panacea. This was to subdivide existing cinemas into three ('tripling', or sometimes two – 'twinning') and to reduce seating levels in each new mini-cinema to current levels of demand. It was calculated by the two major film circuits that the optimum size of a first-run auditorium should be around 600 seats, with two small 'screens' each seating 100–150, mainly devoted to revivals, minority appeal films, or continuing runs transferred from the principal auditorium. In this way an element of choice would be brought back again to attract local audiences, and hopefully persuade them to return to regular patronage. In practice it meant an average Odeon or ABC cinema was reduced in seating from, say, 1500 seats to somewhere about 900 seats in total. The system certainly brought about greater flexibility in the showing of films, and instead of the old rigid policy of booking films in for a week only, they could be retained for as long as audience demand warranted. Thus a few years ago, the film *Towering Inferno* originally booked in for a week, enjoyed such an unexpected box office success in the London suburbs that it was being retained, after transfer to a smaller screen, for as long as six or eight weeks, Closures have continued throughout the late sixties and seventies in order not to overload areas where other cinemas were being tripled. It was an ingenious solution and it has certainly helped to arrest the decline of the cinema, both in terms of audience attendances and building losses.

However, it is difficult to categorise what has happened since the war as other than an unmitigated disaster for the cinema as a building. At the outbreak of war in 1939 it was estimated there were about 5500 cinemas open in Britain; after the war in 1946 this had shrunk to 4714, and to 4483 in 1955. By 1965 the figure had dropped to 1971 and to 1530 in 1975. The rate of closures still outnumber any gains in numbers of auditoria by subdivisions. At the beginning of 1980 the most accurate figure available of cinemas still open stood at 1088. With accelerating closures, and eliminating ethnic minority cinemas, whose progress is often difficult to chart, it seems that less than 1000 cinemas will be open by the end of 1981. The figures in terms of the drop in attendances are even more astonishing: in 1946 there were 1635 million cinema admissions (or 31 million patrons a week), in 1955 this had dropped to 1182; and in 1965 to 327. In 1975 the figure was down to 124 million and in 1980 to under 100 million (or less than two million patrons a week). The table of cinema admissions and takings 1974–7,

As cinemas closed in the sixties, owners sought other appropriate use. The Islington Odeon was used for car parking when required

taken from the *Annual Abstract of Greater London Statistics*, indicates that box office takings have only gone up through steeply rising ticket prices, not through stabilising attendance figures. These prices have gone up far more than inflation, especially in the West End of London, and the time has come when they are proving an active deterrent to attendances other than near the start of the run of a blockbuster film.

For example, in the early 1950s in a suburban cinema, an average front circle seat cost 2/3d, and 1/9d in the rear circle; moreover that entitled the patron to admission to what was frequently a double feature bill lasting approximately 3½ hours. Today a similar seat will cost £1.80–£2.00 for a programme almost invariably consisting of one feature film, and usually lasting little over two hours. Averaging up the early fifties price, making the most generous allowance for inflation through the available price indices, the circle seat today that costs about £2.00 should cost no more than £1.30. Things are even worse in the West End of London where many cinemas have a minimum admission price of as much as £3.00 to all seats. It is therefore a reasonable supposition that as overheads rise and admission prices keep pace with them, ahead of inflation, there is likely to be increasing consumer resistance to paying the prices and, however good the films, there may be a general reduction in attendance figures, accompanied by a sharper drop in the West End as people tend to wait until the films reach the cheaper cinemas in the suburbs and provinces.

**CINEMAS: ADMISSIONS AND TAKINGS 1974–7**

|  | West End (a) | | | Greater London | | | Great Britain | | |
|---|---|---|---|---|---|---|---|---|---|
|  | 1974 | 1976 | 1977 | 1974 | 1976 | 1977 | 1974 | 1976 | 1977 |
|  | (1) | (2) | (3) | (4) | (5) | (6) | (7) | (8) | (9) |
| Number of cinemas | 56 | 52 | 62 | 228 | 235 | 246 | 1,535 | 1,525 | 1,510 |
| Admissions (thousands) | 10,860 | 7,742 | 7,938 | 30,291 | 22,635 | 22,391 | 138,455 | 103,865 | 103,482 |
| Gross box office takings (£ thousands) (b) | 10,404 | 10,084 | 11,977 | 20,012 | 21,544 | 24,303 | 69,338 | 75,829 | 85,546 |
| Seating capacity of cinemas (thousands) | – | – | – | 164 | 139 | 130 | 973 | 827 | 764 |
| Percentage of capacity filled (c) | – | – | – | 19.9 | 17.7 | 17.6 | 21.2 | 18.4 | 18.5 |
| Average price of admission (new pence) | – | – | – | 66.1 | 95.2 | 108.5 | 50.1 | 73.0 | 82.7 |

SOURCE: DEPARTMENT OF TRADE (BUSINESS MONITOR M2)

Note: The figures in the table are derived from annual returns made by cinemas, including news cinemas, open at the end of the year and also those open 26 weeks or more during the year but temporarily closed at the end of the year. They do not include cinemas showing only 16mm film.
(a) Addresses in W1, SW1, and WC2 postal areas.
(b) Includes VAT.
(c) Estimated by dividing the average weekly admissions for the year by the number of complete seat performances (complete performances multiplied by the number of seats).

Access to the box office returns for the year ending February 1976 in respect of seven West End cinemas is revealing.

**BOX OFFICE RETURNS FEBRUARY 1975–FEBRUARY 1976**

| Cinema | Seating capacity | % Audience capacity in year | Box office takings for year | Any special attractions? |
|---|---|---|---|---|
| Carlton, Haymarket | 1,157 | 17.9 | £237,000 | — |
| Rialto, Coventry St | 594 | 21.2 | £116,000 | — |
| Odeon, Leicester Sq | 1,963 | 26.3 | £616,000 | James Bond |
| Leicester Sq Theatre | 1,402 | 40.5 | £667,000 | — |
| Prince Charles cinema | 631 | 49.0 | — | *Emmanuelle* |
| Odeon, Haymarket | 600 | 50.2 | — | *Night Porter* |
| Scene 2, Leicester Sq | 116 | 60.0 | — | *Young Frankenstein* |

It is only to be expected that the highest percentage attendances will be achieved by the smaller cinemas, but two interesting factors emerge from the figures, first that such a well-known and popular cinema as the Odeon, Leicester Square only achieved just in excess of a quarter capacity over a whole year, even with the able assistance of Roger Moore as James Bond, and secondly that even at the larger cinemas, a soft-porn film like *Emmanuelle* or the masochistic *Night Porter* would have had long and highly lucrative runs. This may be a comment on the moral turpitude of London cinema audiences, but on the other hand neither film could have achieved comparable box office success outside London to, say *Grease*, *Close Encounters of the Third Kind*, *Saturday Night Fever*, or *Star Wars*. While it was in the West End, *Grease*, incidentally, created the attendance record at the 1336 seat Empire, Leicester Square with 31,689 admissions in its first week, indicating that the normally slack early afternoon performances were all packed to capacity. The fact that falling cinema attendances have been halted in the last year or two can be confidently ascribed almost entirely to the four films mentioned above, and this is a fair reflection that these films, although not to everyone's taste, were shrewdly gauged to take advantage of what the public wants today by way of entertainment. There are signs also that the cinema corporations continue to be more responsive to audience reactions, as indicated by the success in 1979–80 of the films *Alien*, *The Deer Hunter* and *Apocalypse Now*, all incidentally X-rated. Audiences will soon tire of a surfeit of horror or Vietnam, so where next? Blockbusters are essential for the survival of the cinema; perhaps the Western is due for a revival in the 1980s building on the foundations so securely laid by Sergio Leone in the sixties.

Before examining why the cinema myth developed in the first place, a few more points should be made with regard to the post-war decline. First, bingo halls. There is now good evidence that nearly 20 years after the first cinema was converted into a bingo club, some of the gilt has tarnished on this once burgeoning industry. The very large and luxuriously appointed clubs, like the Tooting Granada, continue to be outstanding successes financially, even allowing for the cost of fitting them out. That the bingo craze has lasted so long at all is cause for astonishment, but the present evidence is that a significant proportion of the older and more shabby clubs are now closing down in the face of falling attendances, membership and competition from the presence of nearby smarter rivals with their bigger prize money, like the Mecca, Top Rank or Granada clubs.

However, it cannot be stressed too highly that bingo halls have proved to be the salvation of many cinemas that would otherwise have been demolished. Cinemas, being basically windowless brick boxes, do not readily lend themselves to conversion without destroying the interest of their internal decorations. Bingo and tripling generally leave the best features intact; warehousing is too heavy and intensive a use for fragile plasterwork to withstand; and any insertion of windows or intermediate floors destroys the essential qualities of a cinema interior.

So far as future projections of cinema numbers are concerned the present EMI/ABC circuit (formed in 1967 when ABC acquired Shipman and King Cinemas) now operate 276 cinemas, or just over half their 1939 figure. It is known that their long-term plans envisage a circuit of about 120 cinemas and a reduction in London from 55 to about 30 cinemas. The Rank Organisation with about 230 cinemas is currently reducing to below 200. Both the main circuits maintain confidential lists of cinemas which are always available for sale or rent. Granada's policy towards their 30 cinemas remains in doubt. They indulge in no widespread advertising, with the result that their catchment areas are more than usually localised. It would be no surprise if they pulled out of cinema-operating completely, and concentrated on those cinemas that are successfully run as bingo clubs. In October 1979 the annual figures from the EMI group showed profits that were so diminished as to put the whole future of their cinema operation in doubt. The Rank Organization's announcement of a withdrawal from film-making prefaced the news in June 1981 that they were closing another 30 cinemas the following autumn, mostly in the suburbs, and even including such a recent arrival as Goldfinger's 1966 Odeon at London's Elephant and Castle. Video and the ever-rising costs of oil to heat cinema auditoria are growing threats to future prosperity.

In the midst of this gloomy outlook, it has to be seriously considered whether tripling existing cinemas has been a successful ploy, or whether it is simply a temporary remedy. From the purely aesthetic standpoint, it is not entirely satisfactory. Most tripling subdivisions are achieved quickly and cheaply by dropping an acoustic wall from the front edge of the circle to the stalls floor, and forming two small studios with a common projection box within the former rear stalls area. The circle then continues to serve as the whole of the seating area for the main auditorium, utilising the original screen. Occasionally the old front stalls seats are retained, but more often they are removed, leaving a clear floor area, and incidentally frequently creating acoustic problems with the increased reverberation periods. In this way it can be admitted that the most interesting decorative features of cinema interiors, such as the auditorium side walls, ceiling and proscenium arch, are usually preserved. Twinning is sometimes achieved by the same technique, but using the rear stalls area as a single studio. More often it is done, provided there is sufficient vertical height and with far more damage to the cinema decorations, by an overall horizontal division through the whole auditorium, thus creating two

Tripling in the raw. Drop wall from circle front creating two small studios under the circle. Front stalls removed. Nothing can disguise the essential quality of a botch-up (Granada, Walthamstow)

approximately equal sections. This more radical approach is occasionally employed for tripling with the lower half divided into two.

However, are these new mini-screens really a satisfactory environment in which to watch a big screen film? Their frequently subterranean location creates a claustrophobic atmosphere, and because the studios and their screens are so small, there is often the slightly uneasy sensation that the experience is not so different from watching a large television in a well-filled drawing room. This is not necessarily a criticism, but it is a long way from the concept of a cinema being a dream palace offering a sense of occasion as a setting for films. It is perhaps understandable that generally speaking the very small studios of today find greater favour with the

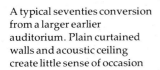

A typical seventies conversion from a larger earlier auditorium. Plain curtained walls and acoustic ceiling create little sense of occasion

younger generation of filmgoers, who only remember the supers in their seedy decline and empty, musty vastness, rather than the older generation who can nostalgically remember their heyday. Also, on a purely practical level, soundproofing inadequacies have often been experienced in the 'triples', and a loss of picture quality caused by central projection from one booth via mirrors, as well as poor sound. The fact remains that tripling of cinemas, and latterly the belated appearance of some films with that sorely missed quality of mass appeal, has at the very least created a breathing space in the decline of the cinema. The major threat of television continues. Since that decisive day in 1953 when a Coronation was televised for the first time, and then with the introduction of a commercial channel in 1955, public awareness has grown of the potential of the medium. A total of 4.5 million television licences in 1955 had grown to 13.2 million in 1965 and 17.7 million in 1975. It will not be long before the total tops 20 million. At the same time television has also been improving, particularly in terms of picture quality, and a decade ago the *coup de grâce* of colour television was administered. All of a sudden there seemed nothing that the cinema could do better; even the once vital appeal of cinemas as a source of bi-weekly visual news coverage has been trumped by television and its daily news bulletins, with the result that we have witnessed the demise of such internationally famous newsreels as Pathé in the last decade.

As cinema audiences have grown smaller, have they grown more discriminating? The answer must be a qualified 'yes', for curiously one of the successes of BBC Television's second channel has been to prove that an audience of two or three million can be captured to watch a reputable foreign film with subtitles, of a sort that would be a box-office disaster outside the rarified atmosphere of West End London. Films in the cinema have undoubtedly improved both in technical quality and in overall entertainment value over the past few years; people will always go to the cinema to see a good film, if for no better reason than they do not want to wait five years for the embargo to expire before it can be shown on television. But even here a cautionary word must be added, for there is an increasing tendency for excellent new films that do not obtain a national release to get an early showing on television. The damaging side-effect of this can only be to prevent more people leaving that fireside armchair to visit the cinema. And, finally, there is the looming threat of home-based video equipment, now on sale at ever-decreasing prices, to enable people to see new films from the comfort of their fireside armchairs.

What was the heady elixir that distilled the potion called movie madness? What cravings engendered the dream palaces? The earth-bound solution was simply the need to escape from the harsh realities of the mundane life outside into a fantasy world where the architectural setting proved worthy of the events being depicted on the screen. As R. W. Sexton and B. F. Betts wrote in 1927 in *American Theatres Today*, 'The masses, revelling in luxury and costly beauty, went to be thrilled by the gorgeousness of their surroundings which they could not afford in their home life'. Going to the pictures in the thirties was an event, and the super cinemas created their own sense of occasion. In a time of depression and mass unemployment, the cinema provided cheap entertainment for the whole family. It was also a form of corporate escapism.

'Movie madness'. A queue in the early thirties waits to hear Garbo talk

Perhaps more than in any other entertainment medium, one can draw conclusions about the direct links between the films of the late twenties and the super cinemas in which they were shown to the adoring public. Without doubt the films created the fantasy cinema interiors to a considerable extent. As films improved in technical quality and scope during the twenties, so did the cinemas. Although silent, the major films of D. W. Griffith and Lubitsch deserved and received appropriate built environments in which to be shown, not to mention Chaplin's no less significant films such as *The Gold Rush* (1925), which enjoyed phenomenal success. With the coming of sound, the talkies both demanded and produced the best from film directors, and within a year or two the buildings were ready to accommodate their work.

Although the generation that grew up between the wars had more choice of entertainment than any other, it was at the same time indiscriminating in its standards, and the subtleties of acting, direction, lighting and other techniques were largely lost upon it during the silent era. This was the explanation for the predilection of directors for the grosser forms of slapstick comedy and 'near-miss' disasters. The coming of sound brought about a transformation of acting styles in the cinema, as well as its buildings, a change, incidentally, that was as fortuitous and fortune-making for Greta Garbo or any movie mogul. The fact that the new films were advertised as 'All Talking, All Singing, All Dancing' plainly demanded a new generation of cinema buildings and unlike America, where the great cinemas were already dying as the Depression approached, British designers responded more than adequately to the expected impetus.

Films like the Busby Berkeley musicals or Cecil B. de Mille's 1934 *Cleopatra* (with Claudette Colbert) find their direct counterpart in the art deco cinema designs of the period. The sets in *Cleopatra* are the classic link: art deco was always strongly biased towards the Egyptian (*vide* Wallis, Gilbert's Hoover Factory in west London 1932–5), and one may point with some justification to a cinema such as the Tooting Granada as the recreation in a working-class suburb of just that unreal quality of an epic film set.

It was into this pattern that when Tooting opened on 7 September

*Provincial Person.* "CAN ANYONE GO IN HERE?"

1931 with Jack Buchanan in *Monte Carlo*, every gimmick possible was brought into play to aid the suspension of disbelief on the part of the audience. For example, by this date technological advance enabled a relatively sophisticated air-conditioning system to be installed, based on cooled air entering the auditorium after being forced through a curtain spray of cold water. Gallons of scent were added to the cold water to produce a delicate aroma of roses, lavender, sandalwood or whatever perfume best suited the happenings on screen that evening. The role of the Mighty Wurlitzer was in the same vein, especially its multitude of special effects. Even its sudden appearance, looming up from beneath the stage with organist already in full flow, was calculated to produce a sense

A typical palm-festooned super cinema foyer of the thirties

of excitement in the minds of customers. Whether this was enhanced by the subsequent renditions of such well-worn and monstrous old warhorses as Ketelbey's 'In a Persian Market' or 'In a Monastery Garden' is open to question. In a cinema such as the Tooting Granada, the flunkeys in the thirties were so numerous as to flank every exit from the auditorium in their pageboy finery throughout every show. If one of them was so unlucky as to suffer the call of nature during the performance, the word had to be passed down for a replacement before he could seek relief.

It was into this air of unreality that audiences of the thirties made their way, to forget the poverty and unemployment outside, and to marvel at the world of make-believe on the screen, for it was the era, unsurpassed since, where films offered a whiff of genuine and wholesome romance, adventure and unreality. In fact just like the cinemas themselves. The greatest attraction was the modest cost, with over three hours' entertainment for as little as 9d. Continuous performances eliminated booking formalities, and as a result one could go to the cinema at any time to suit oneself or on the spur of the moment. Above all, although both films and cinema offered a sense of occasion, one did not, unlike the theatre, have to dress up to go to the cinema; the only person wearing evening dress would be the manager as he stood in the foyer greeting patrons. It was therefore the ideal working-class entertainment, combining and offering escapism with informality, warmth, privacy in the dark, and, most important, cheapness.

Perhaps inevitably, an inverted snobbery grew up about attitudes and addiction to the cinema, as it naturally led to the assumption that films were an uneducative, and thus corrupting, influence on the young. The precise reverse was the case, for not only did the cinema add to experience and perception, it also performed the invaluable service of keeping children off the streets and husbands out of the pubs, with consequent inestimable benefit to the family circle.

Sociologists have sought a link between the fact that in the thirties cinema was promoted as a leisure activity not related to work or education, and yet at the same time it appealed most to the central core of society, the family unit. But the cinema at its peak of popularity could be equally appreciated by the courting couples who sought the warmth and darkness of the auditorium in the absence of being able to afford a car, or enjoy the availability of a convenient living room. Undoubtedly going to the cinema in the thirties (and the buildings were an essential part of that experience) provided both a stimulus and a gratification that was related not only to the psychological state, but also to the social status of the recipient. As David Furnham pointed out in 1972 (in his film *An Acre of Seats in a Garden of Dreams*), there is a distinction between the neutrality and opposition patterns of leisure, and Furnham sees this as applied to the cinema in the thirties. In the neutrality pattern, he sees leisure as a form of relaxation for clerical workers; in the opposition pattern, as recuperation for unskilled manual workers. It was thus no accident that the largest and grandest super cinemas were so cunningly placed within the most densely populated suburbs of lower middle and working-class people, for the cinema represented the first notable cultural victory of the working-class over their betters in society.

The cinema offered a haven of comfort where you could come in out

All part of the show. A thirties photograph of the orchestra that played between films at the Forum cinema in London's Fulham Road

RONALD VICTOR AND HIS OVERTURE ORCHESTRA

The atmosphere of the thirties. The Moderne, Norton on Tees (designed by John Alexander) ready for curtain up on opening night

of the cold, be entertained, have a sleep, have a cuddle, and four hours later be only a few pence worse off. In the world of the thirties cinema, work, family and lesiure became inextricably linked, and that in turn created the movie madness. P. Morton Shand caught the mood exactly in 1930 when he wrote in *Modern Theatres and Cinemas*:

The cinema is primarily a sort of public lounge. It is at once the most public and the most secluded of places . . . One can go alone, à deux, en famille, or in bands. One can take one's children there to keep them quiet, or one can take one's girl there to be quiet oneself . . . One can proverbially filch ideas for a new dress, or 'get off' with one's neighbour. One can enjoy a little nap as easily as the luxury of a good laugh or a good cry. In wet weather it is an escape from the rain, in winter a means of keeping warm. Schoolboys, whose holidays are drawing to a close, know that prevalent epidemics can often be caught there. The cinema is a pastime and a distraction, an excuse for not doing something else or sitting listlessly at home.

And so it was that the super cinemas and the dream palaces played their vital role in fulfilling the popular concept of luxury and creating movie madness and enriching the whole spectrum of life until that 'something else' came along to encourage people to sit 'listlessly at home'. It was television, and now those acres of seats are empty and those gardens of dreams have gone for ever.

# APPENDIX 1
# STATUTORILY LISTED CINEMAS

These cinemas have been statutorily listed by the Department of the Environment as being of special architectural or historic interst.

NB This schedule is complete to July 1981, and indicates that the buildings listed are afforded protection under current planning legislation.

## London

1  Carlton/ABC, Essex Road, Islington, N1. (In use as a bingo club.)
2  Regal/ABC, High Street, Uxbridge, Hillingdon. (Closed at time of writing.)
3  Astoria/Rainbow, Seven Sisters Road, Finsbury Park, N4. (In use as a popular music venue.)
4  Astoria/Odeon, Stockwell Road, Brixton, SW9. (Closed at time of writing.)
5  Cameo-Poly, Upper Regent Street, W1. (Listed only as part of 'blanket' listing of all Regent Street frontages.)
6  Electric, Portobello Road, Kensington, W11.
7  Gaumont, Hill Street, Richmond. (Closed; listed because the cinema is entered through an 18th-century redbrick town house.)
8  Granada, Mitcham Road, Tooting, SW17. (In use as a bingo club.)
9  Granada, Powis Street, Woolwich, SE18. (In use as a bingo club.)
10  New Victoria, Wilton Road, SW1.
11  Spanish City/Odeon, Northfields Avenue, Ealing, W5.
12  Pavilion/Odeon, Shepherd's Bush Green, Hammersmith, W12. (Auditorium subdivided.)
13  Odeon, John Wilson Street, Woolwich, SE18.
14  Plaza, Lower Regent Street, W1. (Listed only as part of 'blanket' listing of all Regent Street frontages.)
15  Palace/Liberty, South Road, Southall, Ealing. (Closed.)
16  Gaumont State, Kilburn High Road, NW6. (Closed at time of writing.)
17  Grosvenor/Odeon, Alexandra Avenue, Rayners Lane, Harrow.

## Elsewhere in England

18  Electric Palace, King's Quay Street, Harwich, Essex.
19  Elite, Market Street, Nottingham. (In use as a bingo club.)
20  Gainsborough, Sudbury, Suffolk.
21  Gem, Great Yarmouth, Norfolk. (Listed mainly for historical associations with C. B. Cochran, as it was where he began in show business when the cinema was built in 1908 and called the 'Palace of Light'.)
22  Gaumont Palace/Odeon, New Canal, Salisbury, Wiltshire. (Primarily listed because the foyer area is the 15th-century great hall of John Halle.)
23  Grosvenor, Oxford Road, Manchester. (Closed at time of writing.)
24  Tower, Anlaby Road, Hull.
25  Rex/Salford, Chapel Street, Salford. (In use as a bingo club.)
26  Odeon, Kings Road, Kingstanding, Birmingham. (In use as a bingo club.)
27  Forum/ABC, Lime Street, Liverpool.
28  Classic, City Square, Leeds. (Listed as part of the 1937 Queens Hotel by Curtis Green.)

29   Odeon, Brentgovel Street, Bury St. Edmunds.

**Wales**
30   Carlton, Oxford Street, Swansea (closed at time of writing.)

**Scotland**
In Scotland, where the listing system is somewhat different, seven cinemas have been statutorily protected by the Scottish Development Department, as follows:
31   Caley, Lothian Road, Edinburgh.
32   George, Portobello, Edinburgh. (In use as a bingo club.)
33   Odeon, Clerk Street, Edinburgh.
34   Playhouse, Leith Walk, Edinburgh. (Closed at time of writing.)
35   Salon, Vinicombe Street, Glasgow.
36   Capitol, Union Street, Aberdeen.
37   Kinnaird, Bank Street, Dundee.

# APPENDIX 2
# GAZETTEER
# OF
# IMPORTANT
# SURVIVING
# CINEMAS

The following list, arranged alphabetically by towns, is restricted to the principal surviving purpose-built cinemas in Britain in 1981. It represents the personal choice of the author.

| TOWN CINEMA | DATE | ARCHITECT/ DESIGNER | PRESENT USE |
|---|---|---|---|
| **Aberdeen** Capitol, Union Street | 1932 | A. Marshall Mackenzie | Cinema |
| **Ashford**, Middlesex Astoria, Church Road | 1936 | David Evelyn Nye | Bingo |
| **Aylesbury** Odeon, Cambridge Street | 1937 | Andrew Mather | Cinema |
| **Bath** Forum, St James's Parade | 1934 | W. H. Watkins and E. Morgan Willmott | Bingo |
| **Beverley** Picture Playhouse, Market Place | 1910 | — | Cinema/ Bingo |
| **Birmingham** Odeon, Birmingham Road, Sutton Coldfield | 1936 | Harry Weedon | Cinema |
| Odeon, Kings Road, Kingstanding | 1935 | Harry Weedon | Bingo |
| **Blackburn** Alexandra Hall, Dock Street | 1909 | — | Cinema |
| **Blackpool** Odeon, Dickson Road | 1939 | Harry Weedon | Cinema |
| **Bognor Regis** Odeon, London Road | 1934 | Whinney, Son and Austen Hall | Bingo |
| **Bolsover**, Derbyshire Plaza | c1912 | — | Bingo |
| **Bournemouth** Odeon, Lansdowne | 1937 | George Coles | Bingo |
| **Brighton** Odeon, St George's Road, Kemptown | 1934 | Andrew Mather | Bingo |
| **Bristol** Odeon, Union Street | 1938 | T. Cecil Howitt | Cinema |
| Whiteladies/ABC, Whiteladies Road | 1921/2 | — | Cinema |
| **Bury St Edmunds** Odeon, Brentgovel Street | 1937 | George Coles | Cinema |
| **Cardiff** New Imperial/Odeon, Queen Street | 1911/ 1936 | William S. Wort (1936) | Cinema |
| **Cheltenham** Gaumont Palace/Odeon | 1932 | W. E. Trent | Cinema |

| TOWN<br>CINEMA | DATE | ARCHITECT/<br>DESIGNER | PRESENT<br>USE |
|---|---|---|---|
| **Chester** | | | |
| Odeon, Northgate Street | 1936 | Harry Weedon | Cinema |
| **Chesterfield** | | | |
| Picture House/Odeon, Holywell<br>Street | 1923 | — | Cinema |
| Regal/ABC, Cavendish Street | 1936 | William R. Glen/<br>J. Owen Bond | Cinema/<br>Pub |
| **Colwyn Bay** | | | |
| Odeon, Conway Road | 1936 | Harry Weedon | Bingo |
| **Deal** | | | |
| Odeon, Queen Street | 1936 | Andrew Mather | Cinema |
| **Dundee** | | | |
| Green's Playhouse, Nethergate | 1936 | John Fairweather | Bingo |
| Kinnaird, Bank Street | 1857,<br>altered | C. Edward | Cinema |
| Picture House, Tayport | c1911 | — | Closed |
| **Edinburgh** | | | |
| Caley, Lothian Road | c1912 | — | Cinema |
| George, Portobello | 1938 | T. Bowhill, Gibson<br>and Laing | Bingo |
| Odeon, Clerk Street | 1930 | W. E. Trent | Cinema |
| Playhouse, Leith Walk | 1929 | John Fairweather | Closed |
| **Exeter** | | | |
| Odeon, Sidwell Street | 1937 | Harry Weedon | Cinema |
| **Glasgow** | | | |
| Salon, Vinicombe Street | 1913 | Thomas Baird, Junior | Cinema |
| Green's Playhouse/Apollo | 1925 | John Fairweather | Cinema |
| **Grays**, Essex | | | |
| State, George Street | 1938 | Frank Matcham & Co | Cinema |
| **Great Yarmouth** | | | |
| Palace of Light/Gem | 1908 | — | Cinema |
| Windmill | 1909 | — | Bingo |
| **Greater London** | | | |
| Astoria, Charing Cross Road,<br>WC2 | 1927 | Verity and Beverley | Closed |
| Astoria/Odeon, Streatham High<br>Road, SW16 | 1930 | Edward A. Stone | Cinema |
| Astoria, Old Kent Road, SE15 | 1930 | Edward A. Stone | Closed |
| Astoria/Rainbow, Seven Sisters<br>Road, Finsbury Park, N4 | 1930 | Edward A. Stone | Pop<br>concerts |
| Astoria/Odeon, Stockwell Road,<br>Brixton, SW9 | 1929 | Edward A. Stone | Closed |
| Bioscope/Biograph, Wilton<br>Road, SW1 | 1905 | George Washington<br>Grant | Cinema |

| TOWN CINEMA | DATE | ARCHITECT/ DESIGNER | PRESENT USE |
|---|---|---|---|
| Capitol/ABC, London Road, Forest Hill, SE23 | 1928 | J. Stanley Beard | Bingo |
| Carlton/ABC, Essex Road, Islington, N1 | 1930 | George Coles | Bingo |
| Carlton/Ace, Green Street, Upton Park, E6 | 1928 | George Coles | Cinema |
| Coliseum, High Street, Harlesden, NW10 | 1912 | — | Cinema |
| Commodore, Stamford Brook, Hammersmith, W6 | 1929 | George Coles | Bingo |
| Dara, Delancey Street, Camden Town, NW1 | 1908 | — | Bingo |
| Dominion, Acton High Street, W3 | 1936 | F. E. Bromige | Bingo |
| Electric, Portobello Road, Kensington, W11 | 1905 | — | Cinema |
| Forum/ABC, Fulham Road, Chelsea, SW10 | 1930 | J. Stanley Beard | Cinema |
| Forum/ABC, Uxbridge Road, Ealing, W5 | 1934 | J. Stanley Beard | Cinema |
| Forum, Highgate Road, Kentish Town, NW5 | 1934 | J. Stanley Beard | Ballroom |
| Gaumont, Tally Ho Corner, Finchley, N12 | 1938 | W. E. Trent | Closed |
| Gaumont Palace/Odeon, Holloway Road, N7 | 1937 | C. Howard Crane | Cinema |
| Gaumont Palace/Odeon, Queen Caroline Street, W6 | 1932 | Robert Cromie | Cinema |
| Gaumont State, Kilburn High Road, NW6 | 1937 | George Coles | Closed Bingo |
| Granada, High Street, Welling, Bexley | 1938 | George Coles/ Komisarjevsky | Cinema |
| Granada, Hoe Street, Walthamstow, E17 | 1930 | Cecil Masey/ Komisarjevsky | Bingo |
| Granada, Mitcham Road, Tooting, SW17 | 1931 | Cecil Masey/ Komisarjevsky | Bingo |
| Granada, Powis Street, Woolwich, SE18 | 1937 | Masey and Uren/ Komisarjevsky | Bingo |
| Granada, St John's Hill, Clapham Junction, SW11 | 1937 | Cecil Masey/ Komisarjevsky | Bingo |
| Grange, Kilburn High Road, NW6 | 1914 | — | Theatre |
| Grosvenor/Odeon, Alexandra Avenue, Rayners Lane, Harrow | 1935 | F. E. Bromige | Cinema |
| Havana/Odeon, South Street, Romford, Havering | 1936 | Kemp and Tasker | Cinema |

| TOWN CINEMA | DATE | ARCHITECT/ DESIGNER | PRESENT USE |
|---|---|---|---|
| Kensington/Odeon, Kensington High Street, W8 | 1926 | Leathart and Granger | Cinema |
| Maida Vale Picture House/Carlton, Maida Vale, NW6 | 1912 | — | Bingo |
| New Victoria, Wilton Road, SW1 | 1930 | E. Wamsley Lewis | Theatre |
| Odeon/Capitol, The Bourne, Southgate | 1935 | Bertie Crewe | Closed |
| Odeon, Claremont Road, Surbiton, Kingston-upon-Thames | 1934 | Joseph Hill | Shop |
| Odeon, Craven Park Road, Harlesden, NW10 | 1937 | Whinney, Son and Austen Hall | Closed |
| Odeon, Denmark Hill, Camberwell, SE5 | 1939 | Andrew Mather | Closed |
| Odeon, Finchley Road, Swiss Cottage, NW3 | 1937 | Harry Weedon | Cinema |
| Odeon, Fortis Green Road, Muswell Hill, N10 | 1936 | George Coles | Cinema |
| Odeon, High Street, Bromley | 1936 | George Coles | Cinema |
| Odeon, High Street, Erith, Bexley | 1938 | George Coles | Bingo |
| Odeon, High Street, Kingston-upon-Thames | 1933 | Adamson, Marshall and Tweedy | Bingo |
| Odeon, High Street, Peckham, SE15 | 1938 | Andrew Mather | Cinema |
| Odeon, High Street, Uxbridge, Hillingdon | 1938 | Andrew Mather | Cinema |
| Odeon, Leicester Square, WC2 | 1937 | Mather and Weedon | Cinema |
| Odeon/Liberty, Balham Hill, SW12 | 1938 | George Coles | Closed |
| Odeon, London Road, Isleworth, NW10 | 1935 | George Coles | Studio |
| Odeon, Powis Street, Woolwich, SE18 | 1937 | George Coles | Cinema |
| Odeon, Rochester Way, Well Hall, SE9 | 1936 | Andrew Mather | Cinema |
| Odeon, Shannon Corner, New Malden, Kingston-upon-Thames | 1938 | George Coles | Factory |
| Palace/Liberty etc, South Road, Southall, Ealing | 1929 | George Coles | Closed |
| Parkhurst, Holloway Road, N7 | 1908 | — | Lecture hall |
| Pavilion/Odeon, Shepherd's Bush Green, Hammersmith, W12 | 1923 | Frank T. Verity | Cinema |
| Pykes/Clifton/New Royalty, Brixton Hill, SW2 | 1910 | — | Sports shop |

| TOWN<br>CINEMA | DATE | ARCHITECT/<br>DESIGNER | PRESENT<br>USE |
|---|---|---|---|
| Regal/ABC, Broadway,<br>Bexleyheath, Bexley | 1934 | Robert Cromie | Cinema |
| Regal/ABC, High Street,<br>Beckenham, Bromley | 1930 | Robert Cromie | Cinema |
| Regal/ABC, Richmond Road,<br>Kingston-upon-Thames | 1933 | Robert Cromie | Cinema |
| Regal/ABC, Streatham High<br>Road, SW16 | 1937 | William R. Glen | Cinema |
| Regal, High Street, Uxbridge,<br>Hillingdon | 1931 | E. Norman Bailey | Closed |
| Regal, Norwood Road, West<br>Norwood, SE27 | 1930 | F. Edward Jones | Closed |
| Regal/Odeon, The Broadway,<br>Wimbledon, SW19 | 1933 | Robert Cromie | Cinema |
| Rialto, Coventry Street, WC2 | 1913 | Hippolyte Blanc | Cinema |
| Richmond/Odeon, Hill Street,<br>Richmond | 1929 | Leathart and Granger | Cinema |
| Royalty/Gaumont, Hill Street,<br>Richmond | 1914 | Sydney W. Davis | Closed |
| Savoy/ABC, London Road,<br>Croydon | 1936 | William R. Glen | Cinema |
| Spanish City/Avenue/Odeon,<br>Northfields Avenue, Ealing, W5 | 1932 | Cecil Masey/<br>Komisarjevsky | Cinema |
| Studios 1 and 2, Oxford Street, W1 | 1936 | Kemp and Tasker | Cinema |
| Troxy, Commercial Road,<br>Stepney, E1 | 1933 | George Coles | Opera<br>Centre |
| Warner, Leicester Square, WC2 | 1938 | Edward A. Stone | Cinema |
| **Guildford**<br>Odeon, Upper High Street | 1935 | Andrew Mather | Cinema |
| **Halstead**, Essex<br>Empire | 1915 | — | Cinema |
| **Harrogate**<br>Odeon, East Parade | 1936 | Harry Weedon | Cinema |
| **Harwich**<br>Electric Palace, Kings Quay<br>Street | 1911 | Harold R. Hooper | Under<br>restoration |
| **Horsham**<br>Odeon, North Street | 1936 | George Coles | Bingo |
| **Hull**<br>Tower, Anlaby Road | 1914 | J. Percival Binks | Cinema |
| **Ipswich**<br>Odeon, Lloyds Avenue | 1936 | George Coles | Cinema |

| TOWN CINEMA | DATE | ARCHITECT/ DESIGNER | PRESENT USE |
|---|---|---|---|
| **Lancaster** | | | |
| Odeon, King Street | 1936 | Harry Weedon | Cinema/ Bingo |
| **Leicester** | | | |
| Odeon, Queen Street | 1938 | Harry Weedon | Cinema |
| **Littlehampton** | | | |
| Odeon, High Street | 1936 | Andrew Mather | Bingo |
| **Liverpool** | | | |
| Forum/ABC, Lime Street | 1931 | A. Ernest Shennan | Cinema |
| **Loughborough** | | | |
| Odeon, Baxtergate | 1936 | Harry Weedon | Bingo |
| **Luton** | | | |
| Odeon, Dunstable Road | 1938 | Andrew Mather | Cinema |
| **Manchester** | | | |
| Corona, Gorton | 1912 | — | Cabaret |
| Greenhill, Cheetham Hill Road | c1911 | — | Bingo |
| Grosvenor, Oxford Road | 1912 | — | Closed |
| Paramount/Odeon, Oxford Road | 1930 | Verity and Beverley | Cinema |
| Rex, Chapel Street, Salford | 1912 | — | Bingo |
| **Middlesborough** | | | |
| Odeon, Corporation Road | 1939 | Harry Weedon | Cinema |
| **Morecambe** | | | |
| Odeon, Thornton Road | 1937 | Harry Weedon | Cinema |
| **Nottingham** | | | |
| Elite, Market Street | 1921 | — | Bingo |
| **Oxford** | | | |
| Picture Palace/Penultimate Jeune Street | 1911 | John R.Wilkins | Cinema |
| Regal/ABC, George Street | 1937 | Robert Cromie | Cinema |
| **Peterborough** | | | |
| Odeon, Broadway | 1937 | Harry Weedon | Cinema |
| **Portsmouth** | | | |
| Majestic/Essoldo, Kingston Cross | 1922 | — | Snooker |
| Odeon, Highland Road, Southsea | 1937 | Andrew Mather | Club |
| Odeon, London Road | 1936 | Andrew Mather | Cinema |
| Palace, Commercial Road | 1921 | A. E. Cogswell | Cinema |
| Savoy/ABC, Kingston Cross | 1937 | William R. Glen | Cinema |
| Shaftesbury/Tatler, Kingston Road | 1910 | — | Bingo |
| **Ramsgate** | | | |
| Odeon, King Street | 1936 | Andrew Mather | Cinema/ Bingo |

| TOWN<br>CINEMA | DATE | ARCHITECT/<br>DESIGNER | PRESENT<br>USE |
|---|---|---|---|
| **Reading**<br>Odeon, Cheapside | 1937 | A. Percival Starkey | Cinema |
| **Redhill**<br>Odeon, Station Road | 1938 | Andrew Mather | 'Busby's'<br>Club |
| **Salisbury**<br>Gaumont Palace/Odeon, New<br>Canal | 1931 | W. E. Trent | Cinema |
| **Scarborough**<br>Odeon, West Borough | 1936 | Harry Weedon | Cinema |
| **Sheffield**<br>Regent/Gaumont<br>Upwell Street | 1928 | W. E. Trent | Cinema |
| **Staines**<br>Regal/ABC, Clarence Street | 1937 | William R. Glen | Cinema |
| **Sudbury**, Suffolk<br>Gainsborough | 1912 | Sidney Naish | Cinema |
| **Swansea**<br>Carlton, Oxford Street | 1914 | Sir Charles Tamlin<br>Ruthen | Closed |
| Castle/ABC, Worcester Place | 1911 | — | Cinema |
| **Taunton**<br>Gaumont/Odeon, Corporation St. | 1933 | W. T. Benslyn | Cinema |
| **Weston-Super-Mare**<br>Odeon, Locking Road | 1935 | T. Cecil Howitt | Cinema |
| **Weybridge**<br>Odeon, Queens Road | 1934 | A. Percival Starkey | Catholic<br>church |
| **Winchester**<br>Regal/ABC, North Walls Road | 1933 | Robert Cromie | Cinema |
| **Wolverhampton**<br>Odeon, Skinner Street | 1937 | Harry Weedon | Cinema |
| **Worcester**<br>Northwick, Ombersley Road | 1938 | John Alexander | Bingo |
| **Worthing**<br>Odeon, Liverpool Road | 1934 | Whinney, Son and<br>Austen Hall | Cinema |
| **Yeovil**<br>Odeon, Court Ash Terrace<br>Central, Church Street | 1937<br>1930 | Harry Weedon<br>— | Bingo<br>Closed |
| **York**<br>Odeon, Blossom Street | 1937 | Harry Weedon | Cinema |

# BIBLIOGRAPHY

Most books concerned with the cinema concentrate on films rather than build-ings, and this list is therefore restricted primarily to those sources of information on actual cinemas found particularly useful in compiling the book.

**Books**
Glasstone, Victor, *Victorian and Edwardian Theatres*, London, 1975
Hall, Ben, *The Best Remaining Seats*, New York, 1961
Howard, Diana, *London Theatres and Music Halls 1850–1950*, London, 1970
Marion, F., *The Wonders of Optics*, London, 1868
Meloy, A. S., *Theatres and Picture Houses*, New York, 1916
Morand, Paul, *New York*, New York
Peart, Stephen, *The Picture House in East Anglia,* Terence Dalton (Lavenham), 1980.
Pildas, Ave, *Movie Palaces*, New York, 1980.
Seaman, L. C. B., *Life in Britain between the Wars*, London, 1970
Shand, P. Morton, *Modern Theatres and Cinemas*, London, 1930
Sharp, Dennis, *The Picture Palace*, London, 1969
Thorne, Ross, *Picture Palace Architecture in Australia*, Melbourne, 1976
*Theatre and Cinema Architecture: A Guide to Information Sources*, Gale Research Co, Detroit, 1978


**Journals**
The most rewarding sources of information are articles in the technical journals, In recent years the following have been especially useful for America:
*Marquee* (Quarterly Journal of the Theatre Historical Society)
*Arts in Virginia* (issue of Fall 1976 by Elroy R. Quenroe, Journal of the Virginia Museum)
'Movie Palaces', *Life Magazine*, 19 February 1971


In Britain, *The Builder, Kine Weekly* and the *Kine Year Books* are invaluable, also the *Cinematograph Times* and *Cinema and Theatre Construction*.


*Pre–1939*
George Coles, 'Modern Cinemas', *The Builder*, 15 and 22 May 1931
'The Curzon Cinema, Mayfair', *Architect and Building News*, 9 March 1934
'The Influence of the Cinema', *Architecture*, September/October 1927
Julian Leathart, 'Auditorium Design in Five Recent Kinemas', *Architect and Build-ing News*, 20 April 1934
Julian Leathart, *Modern Cinema Design*, RIBA Journal, 6 December 1930
'New Victoria Cinema, Wilton Road, London', *Architectural Review*, December 1930
C. H. Reilly, 'The Cinema', *Architectural Review*, August 1935
F. E. Towndrow and Brenda E. Verstone, 'Cinemas and Theatres', special issue of *Architectural Design and Construction*, March 1938
Paul Waterhouse, 'The Shepherd's Bush Pavilion', *Architectural Review*, October 1923
Howard Robertson and F. R. Yerbury, 'The Architecture of Tension', article on Mendelsohn, *Architect and Building News*, 6 December 1929
Stanley D. Adshead, 'The Regent Kinema Theatre, Brighton', *Architectural Review*, November 1921

Robert Atkinson, 'The Design of the Picture Theatre', *RIBA Journal*, June 1921
W. T. Benslyn, 'Modern Cinema Design', *Architects' Journal*, 16 March 1932
'Cinema and Cinematograph', special issue of *Architects' Journal*, 7 November 1935

*Post–1945*
Ian Cameron, 'The Movie Palace', *Sunday Times* Magazine, 21 March 1965
Frederick Bentham, 'A New Vic of 1930', *TABS Journal*, December 1973
Deyan Sudjic, 'Retrospective, the Astoria Finsbury Park', *Building Design*, 1 February 1974
The Quarterly magazine *Focus on Film* frequently provides invaluable research, particularly the Autumn 1975 issue on Odeon Cinemas.
*London Architect* in January and March 1972 carried detailed articles on the New Victoria Cinema by its designer, E. Wamsley Lewis.
Another useful source of information is the news bulletins of the Cinema Theatre Association of 123b Central Road, Worcester Park, Surrey. Anyone interested in cinema buildings should join for the sake of the information distilled and the visits that are arranged to cinemas.
Among local history sources, essential reading is *Cinemas in Portsmouth* by Leslie Bern, May 1975, published by the Portsmouth Reference and Information Centre. Also, *Early Oxford Picture Palaces* by Paul J. Marriott, privately published 1978.
Of several dissertations consulted, one of the most up to date is 'Coming Soon, an Account of Dundee's Cinema Era' by Craig Ross Downie, submitted to the Department of Architecture, University of Dundee in 1979.

## Photographic Acknowledgements

Every care has been taken to ensure credit to the copyright holders of photographs and drawings, but in some cases the illustrations are copies of copies and the names of the original photographers have been lost. Acknowledgements are listed by page numbers, and pride of place must be given to the Greater London Council for permission to reproduce the following illustrations:
Frontispiece, 7, 8, 9, 10 (top), 14, 15 (bottom), 16 (top and bottom), 18, 19 (top and bottom), 20 (top and bottom), 21 (top and bottom), 22, 32–33, 34, 35, 36, 40(3), 41, 42 (top and bottom), 43, 50, 54 (bottom), 58, 78, 79(3), 81, 82 (top and bottom), 94, 95 (bottom), 97, 98 (top and bottom), 99, 101 (right), 102 (top and bottom), 103 (top and left), 104 (top and bottom), 105, 106 (top), 110 (top and bottom), 111(3), 116, 118, 124–125, 128, 129(3), 130, 131 (top and bottom), 132, 133, 134 (top and bottom), 135, 136, 137 (top and bottom), 138 (top and bottom), 139, 146, 149, 150, 152 (top and bottom), 153 (bottom), 154, 155 (left), 157, 160–161, 164, 171 (top and bottom)
National Monuments Record: 1, 87, 90, 91
Sheffield City Library : 23 (top), 24, 25, 51
Ken Powell: 23 (bottom)
J. D. Simson: 26
Gordon Miller: 27, 29
Victor Glasstone: 37, 38, 56 (left), 64 (top and bottom), 69, 70
Brian Mould: 52
Ross Thorne: 65 (top and bottom)
John Sharp: 66–67, 80, 140, 142–143
Martin Sellars: 84–85, 106 (bottom), 107
George Clark: 103 (bottom)

# INDEX

*Names of British cinemas and theatres are shown in capitals*

'. . . treat yourself to a splendidly sympathetic and intelligently written book.' *DAILY TELEGRAPH*

'At last Britain's extraordinary heritage of cinema interiors has had a worthy history written of it.' *DESIGN* MAGAZINE

'. . . heady nostalgic stuff, as well as social and architectural history of a high order.' *THE OBSERVER*

No building type has ever had so swift a rise or so steep a decline as the cinema. Over 5000 were built in Britain between 1900 and 1940. There can scarcely have been a town or a suburb so small as not to rate a cinema of some kind and by 1940 many larger centres had super-cinemas which would seat 4000 or more people. Today less than a third are still showing films, though quite a number have survived, chiefly as bingo halls. In their day cinemas were loathed by architectural critics, particularly for the frankly commercial decoration of their interiors, a quality which we now look at with fresh eyes and a new scale of values.

In this highly entertaining and scholarly book, David Atwell shows how many of these interiors were at best masterpieces of imaginative design, and that even run-of-the-mill ones are an extraordinarily interesting record of popular ideas of comfort and luxury between the wars. While he concentrates on cinema buildings in the United Kingdom, he also discusses and illustrates cinemas in other parts of the world, examining changing moods and fashions in cinema buildings from their giddy heyday to their sad post-war decline. This is an unusual and eye-opening book that makes us re-evaluate a hitherto neglected part of the architectural heritage.

DAVID ATWELL is an architectural historian who has spent most of the last twenty years in conservation work. During architectural training at the Kingston School of Art, he worked in private practice and then in the Historic Buildings Division of the Greater London Council where he was able to expand his researches into cinema and theatre architecture. Now Information Officer for the GLC Architect's Department, he is also a Committee Member of SAVE Britain's Heritage and the Thirties Society. He has appeared many times on television and radio, discussing cinema architecture, and he has written over fifty articles, including a series funded by the British Film Institute, and delivered nearly one hundred lectures on the subject. He is co-author of *Battle of Styles* (RIBA 1975), a study of inter-war architecture in London, and contributed a chapter to *Railway Architecture* (Orbis 1979).

Cover illustration: Auditorium of the Granada, Tooting, before conversion to Bingo. Photograph courtesy of John Sharp

UK Price: £5.95
ISBN 0 85139 773 5
All prices are subject to change without prior notice

THE ARCHITECTURAL PRESS LTD, 9 QUEEN ANNE'S GATE, LONDON SW1H 9BY